ADVENTURES IN AWKWARDNESS

Nicholas Keresztury

PublishAmerica
Baltimore

First printing

All characters in this book are fictitious, and any resemblance to real persons, living or dead, is coincidental.

PublishAmerica has allowed this work to remain exactly as the author intended, verbatim, without editorial input.

Hardcover 978-1-4560-8997-9
Softcover 978-1-4560-8996-2
PUBLISHED BY PUBLISHAMERICA, LLLP
www.publishamerica.com
Baltimore

Printed in the United States of America

TABLE OF CONTENTS

INTRO

Who am I? It is a question I have asked myself since I was a young kid. We live in a society focused on labels and it is how most people define themselves. My name is Nicholas Keresztury. The last name is Hungarian and means "noble" or alternatively "hero to the people." Okay, I made up the second one and perhaps the first one also but I'm sure it's close. I do know the name Nicholas means "Victory". No matter the battle, whether it is with a ferocious hundred-foot giant with razor sharp teeth bleeding deadly acid from every orfus of its body or a moral dilemma, I will not be defeated. Damn, writing about how confident I am scares me. I am 25 years old. I graduated college last year so I suppose I would be labeled a graduate. I thought when I graduated everything would magically come together. The great heavens would open up and I would have all the answers to life's great mysteries. It's like when a climber reaches the top of the mountain and there is no one to meet them. They think: "This is it? Where is the cheering crowd wearing shirts with my face on it, truckloads of balloons, confetti raining from the sky, and the announcer to boom my accomplishments to the world? I want enlightenment damn it!" Upon graduation there were no answers, just more questions and tough decisions. I think every decision I have made in the last five years is a way to delay finally having to join the Real World.

I see myself being pulled towards the inevitable and I dig in my heels hoping to delay it, scratching and clawing at my destiny. Maybe I can run away from it, going on crazy adventures. I think it would be so cool to buy a motorcycle and travel the country with the wind blowing through my hair. Ah, the open road, fresh air, and not a care in the world. When I am burning rubber on my sooped up hog the wind does not travel around me but through me. I have no idea what this means but it sounds deep. I made the mistake of telling my parents that is what I want to do with my life and they were less than pleased. They got so freaked out they dragged me to see every homeless person in town. They said I should sit in the basement in a cardboard box with all the lights off to see what it would feel like. I end up going to graduate school and I continue to ask myself the ultimate question: Who am I?

Physically I am quite the dreamboat, dare I say sexy. Ladies; imagine the sexiest man you have ever seen and I look exactly like him. If you know me personally I most definitely am him. I am relatively tall, just over six feet. My grandmother says I am getting taller every time I see her but I don't have the heart to tell her she is shrinking. Friends would describe me as gangly, more because of my pretention for clumsiness as opposed to my looks. Falling headlong into a trashcan and emerging with a banana on his or her head makes anyone look gangly. If you squint until your vision becomes fuzzy I can say you can grate cheese on my abs. Italian restaurants pay me the big bucks to show off my skills and draw in the ladies. It's quite the living. In truth, I am of average build but with very broad shoulders. I have heard women prefer broad-shouldered men and I do share the characteristic with Bigfoot, which is pretty cool.

Then again, according to the Algonquian Indians, Bigfoot is a descendant of the Witiko. Witikos were cannibalistic giants with supernatural powers, one of which was the ability to possess people and turn them into Witikos. For the record, I don't eat people and can't possess people to create a Nick Keresztury army. I have short dark brown hair but am jealous of those that have long flowing locks. Elvis had the best hair of all time. According to legend he could control it on command, curling it into a tight mass and whipping enemies with it. Once the government discovered his powers he joined a secret task force featuring other singing sensations to eradicate evil wherever it may lie. He joined a shape shifting Cher, a master of disguise Michael Jackson, and Madonna harnessing the power of sex. It was a deadly foursome. When I do grow my hair out long it naturally curls into a thick mop. I am saddened to say besides cleaning floors my hair does not have magical powers.

I have a square face accented by a dark dimple of my left cheek. I have barely swimmable dark brown eyes, by far my best feature. Of course, they are covered by thin-framed glasses. Although I sometimes rock out the jeans my wardrobe of choice is khaki shorts and a polo shirt. For a while, I tried to pull off the cut jeans, rebellious T-shirt, and worn sandals look. For a week I alternated between a shirt that said "I am making a statement" and one that said "The meaning of life is me." Somehow, no one understood the statement I was making. I also have a tattoo on the back of my left shoulder blade. It's pretty awesome. It is a cartoon character of some sort breathing fire and burning down a village but I will leave the details up to the imagination. I figure now that I have a tattoo I have instant badass points. Some people say I look like Stephen Colbert and while I wouldn't call him a stud I take it as a compliment. He has a unique air of sexy sophistication about him and his confidence is alluring. Um…that's what some of my lady friends have said about him anyway. It's curious how when people are asked to describe themselves they always think about the physical.

Metaphorically I have no idea who I am. I wish I were a hippy. I would smoke a lot of grass and then maybe things would make sense. I would sit on my couch munching on week old Cheetos and speculate on the nature of the universe. It seems like potheads have the most fun. They laugh at nothing and truly live in the moment. Marijuana advocates say it helps you think more clearly. My freshman year roommate Marcus, who dropped out of school after failing every class, told me Einstein theorized the concept of relativity when he was particularly stoned one evening. Thomas Newton discovered gravity while smoking a joint. There's no way Benjamin Franklin would have flown a kite in a rainstorm to discover electricity unless he was high on something.

Hmmm, would I be happier if I was actually doing something? I imagine myself working in an office somewhere drinking instant coffee and making idle gossip at the water cooler. I would say things like: "How dare Kevin steal post-it notes!", "That jacket is just not a good look on her", and "Did you know that Peggy went miniature golfing with the boss. She's not even a golfer!" If I was doing something like that I would get so bored. I would end up throwing watermelons off the roof and shooting Nerf guns at people. I definitely have to be doing something I really enjoy and find valuable. The real question is whether I can be lazy and do nothing while still contributing something to this world? Balance the two and my dreams and inspirations are fulfilled.

I have been thinking about these questions for some time. It all started when I was ten years old. On a briskly cold November day before my Saturday ritual of watching morning cartoons, breakfast made me think. I brought out a box of Lucky Charms to start my day off right, but my dad said I needed something healthy and more satisfying. I watch the box longingly as he plops a heaping spoonful of porridge into my bowl. This is cruel and unusual punishment. I would say this was 'gruel' and unusual punishment but I'm not a fan of puns. I wonder if Leprechauns eat a lot of cereal and if so are they allowed to eat more than Lucky Charms? I have to admit at age ten I really wanted a Leprechaun. They are rather spunky and oh so cute.

I thought if I followed a rainbow I would find an entire colony of them putting gold in pots and dancing merrily. I would adopt all of them on the spot and bring them home with me. I could tell people instead of imaginary friends I played with Leprechauns. I start to compare Leprechauns to myself when I suddenly have an epiphany. Leprechauns know their purpose from birth. You don't see any working on cars as mechanics or operating on people. I wouldn't trust one with a knife. They don't have to go through years of schooling only to be even more confused about what they want to do. I wish I knew exactly what I was supposed to do with my life or who I was supposed to be. I look to my dad for help.

"Dad, who am I?"

He doesn't look up from his paper. He reads the paper every Saturday after breakfast. He doesn't like to be interrupted but this is a topic I am particularly interested in. I am feeling insecure as of late and felt I would have a better understanding of my life if I discovered an answer to the ultimate question.

"You're a monkey, now eat your porridge."

I must add dear reader that I hate porridge and wonder why I keep eating it. Oliver Twist and his hapless gang of orphans ate such mush and they were well…poor. I like money and I want to make lots of it some day. I dream of having so much money I bath in it just for fun, paper cuts be damned. When I was younger my hero was Scrooge McDuck, so rich he had piles of gold coins stored away in a vault. When I was five I wondered why more ducks didn't own large mansions. I figured the ducks that I saw wandering around the pond in town were just poor and homeless. I felt bad for them. It is unfair they have to wander around poor and alone when a pompous elitist duck is hogging all the wealth. Not to mention the duck thinks he's so special he doesn't have to wear pants. The children's cartoon show was definitely promoting indecent exposure and when kids around the country refuse to wear pants they know who is at fault.

Not to mention McDuck can dive into piles of coins without getting hurt. I have it on good authority that is simply not the case. The other problem I have with Orphans is they wear those goofy little sideways hats. How did those hats become trendy anyway? Those stupid beatniks wear those hats, drinking cappuccino out of tiny cups with their pinkies up. They write poetry they think is "deep". Anyone who reads "save my soul poetry" in one of those hats is not as cool as they think they are. I want to scream at those stupid people at open mic nights that their soul is nothing like a broken oyster and they should admit that no one will ever love them. I figure that would be rude.

"I don't understand dad. I don't feel like a monkey. Why don't I have a tail and fur? The monkeys at the zoo make all these weird noises and fling their own poo."

Dad puts down his newspaper and glares at me. He always reads the sports section and rambles about how athletes are getting paid too much. He's really just mad he never made it to the pros. He played rugby in college and apparently was quite good. As legend has it, meaning he tells the story every night at the dinner table, when he visited Australia to play in a tournament despite a broken leg he had the winning score. Sometimes when he tells the story he has a broken leg and a broken arm or maybe two broken legs. Once when he had drunken a little too much scotch he told me he was paralyzed from the legs down and had to drag himself on his arms to score. The worst part of it all was I believed him, wondering how he had made such a wonderful recovery. I bragged to my friends at school of my dad's accomplishments but they still gave me swirlies. They were just jealous.

"You're a monkey damn it! It's called evolution. Wait; don't tell me you haven't learned about this in school yet. I am gong to call your teacher and have a word with her."

"But…I don't understand dad."

"Think about it this way, maybe in a former life it was you that flung the poo?"

I pause to think. I wonder if other people do it and I am not old enough to realize it. Maybe I am just more sophisticated. Nah, none of this makes sense.

"What does that mean? Dad, I just don't know…what I am supposed to be?"

My dad looks at me. On the outside he looks calm and collected but in his head he is cursing. He assumes the best way to answer this is to talk about sex. Was this the appropriate time for the "talk"? My dad had practiced having this conversation in the mirror but it always ended badly. The more he talked the more confused he would get and he would end up having questions of his own. If I were indeed ready the explanation would have to be handled delicately.

"Son, your mom and I…we got married because we were in love. You see it's complicated. We…did this thing…"

"What do you mean?"

Oh boy my dad thinks. Maybe he could tape record a well thought out speech and play it at just the right moment. There would be no awkward explanations and hopefully no follow up questions. Wasn't he too young to be thinking about this anyway my dad thinks? My dad needed an explanation that would work until I was older.

"A stork…"

"What's a stork?"

"It's a bird. A stork dropped you off on our doorstep. You were wrapped in a cloth and placed in a basket."

"You said I was a monkey. Now I'm a bird. "

I would rather be a monkey than a bird. Monkeys may fling their own poo but they can be smart. I went to the zoo in Washington D.C. and saw Bobo the monkey solve the Rubik's cube in less than a minute. That damn thing gives me a headache. After the monkey solved the cube, Bobo looked directly at me and frowned. He then proceeded to make loud farting noises. The monkey was clearly mocking me. Despite Bobo's rudeness, I have always wanted a talking and singing monkey. I would lead it around school and it would break into spontaneous tuneage. Birds on the other hand just repeat what they hear and fly into windows. They are clearly uncoordinated and can't think for themselves.

"No, No. You're not really a monkey. You were once a monkey. I know it doesn't make much sense now, but…"

"So I turned into a bird. That's awesome. I always wanted to be a dragon and breath fire. Why couldn't I be a dragon baby?"

"A what?"

"Wait; if I was a monkey, then a bird, and am now a human are you saying I can shape shift into other creatures. That goes against everything we have been taught in class but sounds cool."

My dad sighs. Hmmm, there had to be a better way. Apparently my grandparent's never talked about sex to my father although that was more common in those days.

"Let's go into the living room."

Dad sits on the couch and I sit across from him on the Lazy boy. There is an awkward silence as my dad stares at me. He crosses his arms and furrows his brow. I feel like I am about to be yelled at. I have no idea what is going on but he is making me uncomfortable. He smoothes his pants and clears his throat.

"This is a tough topic but I believe you are mature enough to talk about it. I am going to tell you about the birds and the bees..."

"You mean a stork."

"What, no."

"You told me the bird that brought me here was a stork."

"No, no. Okay, there is no Stork."

"Well, what happened to it? Where did the bees come from?"

"Just forget about the bees. Let's start over."

Dad is getting frustrated. He now knows it was probably a mistake to talk about sex with me at such an early age. The stork explanation is obviously not working. He wants to be direct and leave it at that but that might be hard to grasp. Dad breathes out heavily.

"Okay, I'm going to level with you...your mom and I got together...you know, physically. Wonderful things happened and you came along."

"Wonderful things? What do you mean?"

"Your mother and I had...okay, you were inside your mother and...uh...that sounds weird. You should talk to your mother about this."

More confused than ever I go to my mom for guidance. I find her in the laundry room putting laundry into the washer. She doesn't look pleased.

"None of these socks match. There are tall ones, small ones, and ones with different logos. There are not two socks alike. I bought you new ones last week. How does this happen?"

My mom is usually a calm person. Her philosophy is getting all worked up over something never accomplishes anything. Contrary to her philosophy laundry makes her angry. Mismatched socks send her into a tizzy. I once made the mistake of telling her they were just socks and nothing to get mad about. Smoke started coming out of her ears and then her head exploded.

"Mom, I have a question for you. I just don't understand who I am?"

"How many socks total do you think this is? I just don't understand where they all go. It's like the spoons in this household. Somehow we don't have anymore. We have forks, knives, and pretty much every other utensil known to man yet somehow we never have any spoons. They all magically disappear. You know how much I like soup, yet I am afraid if I make it I won't have a spoon to eat it with. It's madness."

Mom takes a deep breath and smoothes her apron.

"Honey, I don't mean to get so upset. What did you ask?"

"I'm just not sure who I am supposed to be."

"You can be whatever you want to be/"

"So I can be a dragon?"

"Well, I don't think..."

"Sweet!"

Wow, I think, that sounds great. I have dreamed about being a fire-breathing dragon, protecting a castle with a wide moat and turrets stretching high into the sky. In the highest tower is a fair maiden locked away in the tallest tower. It is my duty to protect her from the evils of the world. I would say the many soldiers that manned the castle could do it but I ate them. An empty stomach outweighs a heavy conscious. This is probably not what my mom is referring to though. I decide to rephrase the question.

"But, I don't know my place in this world."

"Well, what is your dream job?"

I have never understood why people are always so focused on their jobs. I am struggling with identity and a job is just a small part of that. I realize now that my job is not what defines me as a person. When I was ten though, my mom's question did make me think.

"Well, I think being a firefighter would be neat"

"See there you go. It's a very noble job and I think you would be great at it, carrying big hoses and fighting fires. If that's...

"No, not a real firefighter. A Lego firefighter."

"What?'

"Or Lego Batman. I haven't really decided yet. Or I could be a Lego pirate commanding my own ship and getting advice from my own Lego parrot."

My mother looks puzzled. I haven't seen this look since I was three and I stuck a cooked carrot up my nose. I had to go to the emergency room so they could remove it. By the time a doctor saw me it was the wee hours of the morning and the carrot had to be removed with large tweezers. It was quite the ordeal. I'm not really sure why I did it. I could have been jealous of the attention my sister got and I did it so my parents would notice me. I believe I simply missed my mouth and got confused. My parent's have been helping me find my way ever since but in that moment I helped my mom realize something.

I didn't need to plan ahead for the future and decide so early on what I wanted to do with my life. Childhood is a precious thing.

"You're young. Right now just enjoy being a kid."

I realize she's right. I am young and I should live in the moment. Things were different when I was a kid. I felt little pressure to think about the future. My immediate concerns were what size Slurpee I wanted or where my sister kept her diary. I'm 25 now and the innocence of childhood has passed. Some things don't change though. I'm still as confused as I was when I was ten. I'm not sure what the perfect job for me is and I wonder if that's a trap. I mean no job is perfect and I don't need a job to make me happy. Even though I'm in school a part of me feels empty. What do I want and more importantly do I have the courage to go after it. I ask you to come on a journey of self discovery with me dear reader. I will attempt to explore the moments and experiences that make me who I am today through my memories of the significant time periods in my life. The experiences cover different periods of my life, starting with childhood and ending with where I am today. I don't offer epiphanies or even truth. I simply offer a portrait of a man exploring whom he is in the memories that have shaped his life.

CHILDHOOD

DAMN GIRL SCOUTS

I believe elementary school and middle school have a huge effect on a child's development. The curriculum studied inside the classroom is important, but the real development happens in the interactions with others; including classmates, teachers, girls, and even no-good principles. Children learn to express themselves and develop a self-identity. My memories of school seem to run together as if they all happened at the same time. One in particular; however, stands out above them all and was a real turning point for me. Things were different after the "incident". In essence my dad punched my principal in the face. It all started one faithful day during my first period history class. I am listening to Mr. Shank drone on and on about the start of the New World and I am getting antsy. I have never liked him. He has long, thin brown hair that snakes its way down past his shoulders. He ties it back in a messy ponytail. I am pretty sure he highlights his hair to hide the grey but he isn't fooling anyone. He sports a clean-cut goatee that looks a lot greyer than his hair. He wears thin-framed glasses that make him look older than his age. He looks like a starving artist who lives in a run down studio apartment. I see him flirting with the school nurse during lunch and it sickens me. Mr. Shank tucks lose hair behind his ears and lowers his eyes because I guess he thinks it will make him look sexy. He lowers his voice an octave to make it sound more gravely like Clint Eastwood.

I want to tell him that he will never be a suave bad boy but I keep it to myself. Truth be told the lunch lady gives me large portions during lunchtime and I am concerned those extra portions will go to Mr. Shank. I am sitting in class not paying attention. The man is so incredibly boring and he thinks he is a genius. Every so often I glance over at Elizabeth sitting several rows over. I have a major crush on her and am trying to work up the courage to ask her out. We make eye contact but I quickly look away. My plan is to play it coy. We are learning about the first thanksgiving, something about Native Americans and Pilgrims coming together to eat and learn to appreciate their differences. I have seen the Disney animated classic Pocahontas. Not only did I learn raccoons can talk but it is really love that brought Native Americans and Pilgrims together. Sure, juicy turkey topped with gravy tastes pretty damn good but I refuse to believe an awkward looking flightless bird can heal hurt feelings. Maybe add some stuffing and homemade cranberry sauce but it doesn't make up for anger between both sides. I mean my family thanksgivings are always a good time but even then there is the occasional awkward conversation. My father has now become a full-fledged atheist and goes to weekly meetings. When the topic came up at last year's thanksgiving my grandmother on my dad's side was less than pleased.

"Dad isn't there some atheist meal you have to go to."

Dad glares at me. He talks under his breath.

"Shut up."

He looks at my grandmother and smiles.

"He doesn't know what he's talking about. It is just a friendly group that freely discusses religion. I'm not an atheist."

"You better not be. That's not how I raised you", granny chimes in, "I'll sick the wooden spoon on you and make you kneel on corn."

My dad grew up catholic and being an atheist would be quite a shock to my grandmother. My grandmother was the chief disciplinarian in the household. When my father misbehaved he got a wrap on the knuckles with a wooden spoon. She even threatens me with it sometimes and I can't help but laugh. I'm not sure whether it's her short stature or her eye patch. Somehow the eye patch switches eyes inexplicably. I look away for one second and things have suddenly changed. Don't ask about the corn. All I can say is uncooked kernels really get the point across. The meal always ends in a downer when catholic grandma says with a frown that this will probably be her last Christmas. Everyone grows quite and the dinner devolves into the two grandmothers comparing their ailments.

The more Mr. Shank talks about the concept of Thanksgiving the more I question what he is saying. He makes it sound like all the unhappiness and unrest ended quickly and everything were fine. It sounds preposterous to me so I raise my hand like the smart teenager I was.

"Yes, Mr. Shank. So you're saying that they simply put aside all their differences to share a meal together. I think that is a load of bull crap"

Mr. Shank puts down his chalk and stares at me. I am already labeled a troublemaker. I put tacks in his chair once. He jumped up surprised and gave a little squeal. I thought it was funny but the principal told me laughing at someone else's pain was inappropriate. I graduated to spitballs and I got detention.

"Nicholas, that is not appropriate language. We are talking about history here. It's not an opinion. It's fact."

"So are you saying that if the Nazis and the Jews had sat down over some bread and hummus there would have been no problem and everyone would have skipped off into the sunset?

The Nazis would have still waged war against the Jewish people. It's not opinion. It's fact."

The vein in his head bulges. I think I am being clever even if no one in the class really has any idea what I am talking about. My dad studied history in college and World War II is of particular interest to him.

"May I remind you Nicholas that I am Jewish and I find that comment offensive"

I should stop here. Mr. Shank hates me and my reputation for being a classroom distraction will not help my case. I could apologize and get off easy but that is not my style.

"Think about the Nazis. They would have to eat hummus. That stuff is gross."

An hour later I sit in Mr. Turnball's, the principal, office with my parents. I look around at the pictures on his wall. He has a picture of himself shaking hands with president George W. Bush. Mr. Turnball looks happy and is giving thumbs up to the camera. The slight frown on the president's face says it all. Another picture is of him and the guy who played Mr. Belding on 'Saved by the Bell'. Mr. Turnball claims he got a drink with his hero at a bar in Pittburgh and beat him in a game of darts. I spot a Mr. Belding bobblehead on his desk and my smile slowly turns into a look of horror.

"Mr. and Mrs. Keresztury, Nick has a problem with authority. This is not the first time he has had an issue with Mr. Shank. Just last week Sam wrote some rather inappropriate things on the chalkboard before class. He wrote: "Mr. Shank has a microscopic penis" and "Mr. Shank smells like poo."

My dad tries to suppress a laugh and even my mom smiles. Mr. Turnball frowns and narrows his eyes. He clears his throat and continues.

"He has had problems with other teachers as well. In biology class he was supposed to dissect a frog. He claimed he was an animal rights activist and his morals were being threatened."

"You know the polar bear is losing its habitat, exploited by greedy people like you."

"Yes, well…the point is Mrs. Keresztury this is unacceptable behavior. He then put a frog in Mary Willomer's locker and one in her backpack."

"Serves her right. She is a horrible person."

My dad doesn't mince words. He says honesty is the most important quality a person can have but I question that now. If I go around telling people exactly how I feel there would be chaos. There would be no stopping me. I would be universally hated across the school. Although you know what, it would be fun. I would tell hopeless romantics that love doesn't exist and they were just plain hopeless. I told a dog I loved it once. The dog stared at me for a second, licked its privates, and left the room. Now that's rejection. I decided right then and there that love was a fleeting concept. Mr. Turnball sighs heavily.

"Okay, I'm not even going to ask why…"

"She's a girl scout."

Mr. Turnball is losing his patience. He always thought parents had an influence on their child but this was getting ridiculous. He wonders what lessons are being taught at home.

"And? Is that it? Are you saying that she is a horrible person because she is a girl scout? It is a great organization that teaches young ladies responsibility and leadership. My daughter is a girl scout."

"That explains a lot", my dad says stone faced.

"Excuse me."

I look at my dad knowing there is going to be fireworks. He is the most stubborn man I have ever met and he is not going to back down. My mother grabs his arm to try and calm him down but his eyes have narrowed.

"They wear those nice uniforms and sell cookies door to door. I love thin mints but do they really have to charge nearly five dollars a box. I could buy them at half the price somewhere else but do I really want to tell the nice girl in pigtails I won't buy anything. What if she goes home and cries to her mother? I have ruined her day and that's the kind of guilt I don't want. It's called extortion and you have the nerve to support it!"

Mr. Turnball is fuming but he is trying to suppress his anger. I sit back in my chair hoping things will calm down. I look to my mom but she has her head down. Trying to stop a speeding locomotive is impossible with just words. Luckily Mr. Turnball leans back in his chair and puts his hands behind his head. There is a pause as Mr. Turnball studies my dad.

"Do you know the meaning of Pi sir?"

My dad looks puzzled.

"Isn't it some kind of math thing?"

"Yes, the concept is taught in math classes across the state. I'm guessing you are not an educated man so you probably don't know that Pi is equivalent to 3.1416 and lots of numbers after that. The point is I feel the number is confusing. Upon my recommendation the school board ruled the math concept of Pi should be rounded up to 4 from now on. If you think about it 3.1416…is an uncomfortable number."

My dad clenches his fist. My dad did graduate but he himself says he should have gotten a degree in perpetual underachievement with a concentration in the art of laziness. He says I should learn from his mistakes.

"What does that have to do with my son?"

"Power", Mr. Turnball says, getting up from his desk and walking to the window, "You see, I can kick Sam out of school for the rest of the semester if I see fit. Believe me, the school board would have no problem with the decision. Don't tempt me Mr. Keresztury?"

My dad gets up and points a finger in Mr. Turnball's face.

"Listen here, do not threaten me or my son."

"How dare you talk back to me in my office. You are by far the rudest man..."

This is where things get out of hand dear reader. I watch in horror as my father leaps across the desk and tackles Mr. Turnball. They wrestle around on the floor screaming at each other.

"I can see where your son gets it."

"Oh okay, maybe I should just sell my soul to satin for a cookie."

My mom and I stand there watching what is happening, not sure exactly what to do. Years later when I become obsessed with professional wrestling I think back to this fight. All my dad needs is way to tight stretchy pants and a cape. He would have long stringy hair and a skull and crossbones tattoo on his back. I imagine my dad body slamming Mr. Turnball and hitting him in the back with a chair. Man that would be awesome. My dad pushes my principal into the window in his office looking out onto the playground. Mr. Turnball watches in horror as dozens of fifth and sixth graders gather around to watch the festivities. A murmur runs through the crowd and the children start cheering on my dad. A voice can be heard above the fray.

"Kick his butt. Destroy him. Show him who's really the boss."

Mr. Turnball's face is smushed against the window and he has to yell out of the side of his mouth.

"I know that's you Miss Armstrong. I will deal with you after school."

I start to think that the fight is just between two middle-aged men taking out their feelings of inadequacy on each other when my dad climbs on top of Mr. Turnball, pins him to the ground, and punches him in the face.

All I remember afterwards is all the chaos. Mr. Turnball's secretary, coming in to the office just in time to see the punch, temporarily losses her mind and pulls the fire alarm. The sprinklers go off and students and teachers alike pour into the hallways. There is yelling and confusion as the building is evacuated. I stand there shocked as Mr. Turnball pushes my dad off of him and struggles to his feet. There is a large bruise around his eye. His shirt is wrinkled and there is a tear on the sleeve. Water from the sprinklers is pouring down all around him. By this time his suit is soaked.

"Look what you have done. This is a tailored suit. It's irreplaceable. Get out of my school!"

"Okay, this has gotten out of hand", my dad says, getting up, "I'm sorry."

Outside the window I can see fire trucks pull up and fire fighters run into the building hefting gigantic hoses. Things are quickly getting out of hand.

"Oh, now you're sorry. Do you have any idea what you have done? You are going to make this right. I am not going down for this."

The police are called and statements are taken. The teacher Mr. Shank tells the authorities I am an anti-semite and a racist. After being questioned I admit to not liking people who wear kilts without a good reason. They look like skirts to me and fat men look awkward in them. It's a tradition and I respect that but it can be taken too far. If it were a tradition in my family to run around the neighborhood naked I would only do it when appropriate. I also admit I don't like Italian food or Swiss cheese. My father was less than pleased when he had to take anger management classes. I have to say it kind of worked.

My dad was kinder and gentler although it took some time. Right after the "incident" my dad still blamed Mr. Turnball for things that weren't his fault. The toaster burnt his toast.

"I set it on light browning. I bet that no good principal of yours hates toast. I'll light HIM on fire."

"Dad, that seems a bit harsh"

"Harsh, harsh! He bit me and quite frankly he bruised my ego. He hurt my feelings."

A week later the dryer shrinks his lucky boxers, the black silky ones with red hearts on them that my mom bought my dad for Valentine's Day many years ago. He also got a big black pillow in the shape of a bomb that says "Sex Bomb" on it. It was the day I was conceived. The fact that I know this disturbs me, as does the fact that my mother tells me this over the breakfast table all the time as if I could ever forget the story.

"What am I going to do? I can't wear these. They cut off my circulation. Man, my luck is going to change and horrible things will start to happen. Oh my god, I have great sex every time I wear these. I bet that no good principal of yours has something to do with this. He wants me to be uncomfortable, unlucky, and sexless."

"That seems a bit extreme dad."

"You'll understand when you're older"

"I'm in high school. I know what sex is"

"Good. Your mother says I still have a lot to learn."

Mr. Turnball takes a period of leave without pay. No one is exactly sure what he did with his break but there are plenty of rumors. Robert Avery claims he saw Mr. Turnball sleeping on a bench in the park sporting a scruffy beard and wearing a crumpled suit. I thought I saw him outside of the post office asking for change but I figured I was imagining things. For a time I thought it would be cool to be homeless. Oscar the

Grouch lives in a trashcan and he is so cool. He may be angry and looks like a monster but under all of that green puppet fuzz he has a kind heart. A good therapist and a drink every once in a while and he would be fine. On a side note, I always had a lot of questions about all the Sesame Street characters. When Elmo is tickled he giggles but doesn't he get tired of it and when I do that to the ladies why do they tell me to stop? I have also always wondered where Muppets come from. Are they asexual and an entirely different creature, like fuzzy aliens or do they have Muppet parents. Imagine if Oscar the Grouch and Miss Piggy got together. That would be one ugly Muppet baby.

Regardless, I don't believe Robert. I also heard Mr. Turnball went to Florida to work off some anger. He allegedly went to the Everglades and wrestled a crocodile. This seems a bit preposterous and quite frankly I am not impressed. If it were a bear then I would have to give the man some props. I have heard stories about how they eat campers and of course they steal picnic baskets. They claim Smoky the Bear prevents forest fires but for some reason he's always around when they happen. Let me tell you, I would never give a bear a box of matches. My favorite rumor comes from Edna, the old lunch lady who wears a goofy hairnet and smells like aged cheddar cheese. I really can't say anything bad about Edna seeing she always gives me an extra scoop of mashed potatoes. During the big food fight last year she gave me the extra hard week old rolls. She claims Mr. Turnball went to Vegas and lost the rest of his dignity gambling and well…partaking in extra curricular activities with a nice young woman named Candy. In reality he spent most of his time on his couch watching T.V., eating chicken wings, and drinking boxed wine. Sounds great to me.

As for me I became quite the celebrity as the guy that got Mr. Turnball suspended. The jocks give me a high five every time I pass them in the hallway. By the end of the day my hand aches so instead they playfully punch me in the stomach. They really do underestimate their own strength. They ask me to join their crew but half the time I can't understand what they are saying. Some of them just grunt and call it speaking. I wonder what the girls see in them. The Goth kids invite me to a party with fire dancing and some kind of prayer ritual. Upon arrival I am unclear on whether they are going to worship me as a god or sacrifice me. In the end we end up roasting marshmallows and making Smores.

When one of the girls named Erin wearing all black starts crying about how her boyfriend dumped her I am pretty sure I am in the Twilight Zone. I date Erin for a while but she claims my birthday is a sign of the apocalypse and we break up. Some of the cuter girls in my class give me extra attention. Every time I see them in the hallway they smile and wink at me. I think they view me as a rebel. Women love a bad boy. The nerds obsessed with Magic Cards and Dungeon and Dragons give me nerd bumps. Just for clarification a nerd bump is when someone gives a weak fist pound and gives you a typical Elfish greeting. I have no idea what they are saying but man those guys are awesome.

Mr. Turnball comes back and I am on my best behavior. There was no way I want to get in trouble again and have another parent conference. I do all my class work and don't argue with the teachers. I am especially well behaved in Mr. Shank's class. I come in extra early and always tell him good morning. I even brought him coffee once. He had another kid in the class drink it to make sure it wasn't poisoned. It really freaks him out and he stares at me during class. He thinks I am plotting something. Sometimes I see Mr. Turnball in the hallway and I give him a nod. It's like there is an unspoken agreement between us that what happened does not need

NICHOLAS KERESZTURY

to be mentioned again. The cold stare he gives me when he first returns after some time turns into a nod and eventually a slight smile. Whether it is forced or not I appreciate it. The outpouring of attention I got from the students soon dies away and I am just a normal kid again. Some of the kids still give me nerd bumps but I think it's just because they want me to join their Dungeon and Dragon's group. They are always looking for more dwarfs.

When I think about who I am and what has shaped my life this is one of the first things I think about. I was a troublemaker. I acted up in class and thought I was being cool. At home I'm pretty sure I drove my parents nuts. A week before the school incident I shoved pizza dough in the family VCR and it broke. I was punished and my parents had to buy a new one. Out of spite I did it again. When I was asked why I did it I stubbornly responded that no one could tell me what to do. Let's be honest, I was a handful. The incident at the school taught me a very important lesson. My actions have consequences. I stopped acting up in school and became less of a tyrant at home.

THE SCREAM HEARD FOR MILES

In elementary school I was assigned to give a five-minute presentation on who my hero was. I remember being very confused. What was a hero and what were the personal characteristics they must display? The examples cited in class were George Washington and Oprah Winfrey. George Washington may have led the continental army to victory in the Revolutionary War and been the First President of the United States but didn't he chop down his father's cherry tree. Maybe it makes sense if he had needed firewood immediately or had an intense disdain for cherries but where is the reasoning behind that? Not to mention he had false teeth. This confused me at the time. Every time I go to the dentist I am told dental hygiene is very important. The man is supposed to be some great military leader even though he can't take the time to brush and floss. Don't even get me started on Oprah. Okay, she does some great things, I give you that, but it's scary how big she is. With the amount of influence she has on popular culture you could argue she is more powerful than Jesus. Relax, I simply mean in terms of popularity. I mean if she promotes anything on her show sales skyrocket. She even has her own book club. Jesus doesn't have his own book club. I wonder if he reads a lot. The bible is pretty thick but where does he find the time. I can imagine Jesus with a show like Oprah's.

"Welcome to today's show. There is a book I think we should all read, a book written by a real pal of mine, the bible. Before we get to that we have a special guest that came a long way to visit us this evening. Please welcome, God"

The studio audience claps politely.

"Thank you, delighted to be here."

As he speaks the audience listens intently. It turns out he has a somewhat dry sense of humor. He jokes that every so often him and the devil sit down for a game of chess. If he wins he gets to save an old man from drowning or prevent a plane's engine from malfunctioning. Sometimes they play Monopoly but Satin always seems to win. God suspects Satin steals money when he isn't looking. Truth be told Satin has a propensity to cheat and God always gets upset and storms off in a huff. How else do you explain earthquakes? He is also a big sports enthusiast. Every year he takes a vacation by sailing around the world. Every so often he takes an extended vacation, which explains the plague and the popularity of Tickle me Elmo's. The conversation becomes uncomfortable when God starts to give Jesus fatherly advice.

"God, you are such a great guest."

"Maybe that's because I am your only guest. Do you not find it the least bit ironic that your show is on comedy central? Where's the self-respect? You are not even winning you time slot."

"Yeah, but my show is more popular than the dark one. When the king of the underworld started that late night talk show with death as his sidekick there were very poor ratings."

"That's because death kept accidentally touching the guests and killing them. The show was cancelled after a week."

Jesus smiles. The reason for cancellation may be true but Jesus knows his show at least had stayed on the air longer and has more viewers.

"It still counts."

"Of course, every time we play chess Satin will not stop whining about his stupid show and death screwing everything up. He said he tried to get death fired but death kept threatening to touch him. Man, Satin will not let things go."

Jesus looks down at his cue cards, trying to think of what to say next. This wasn't as easy as Jesus thought it would be.

"Well, I'm not really sure what to ask now."

God sighs

"See, you are no Oprah."

"But…that hurts my feelings."

"And you should cut your hair hippy. You look like the drummer for an 80's hair band."

Jesus looks dejected. He runs his fingers through his long golden hair. He spends every morning extensively shampooing and conditioning. Jesus takes pride in his hair and let's just says it brings in the ladies. Why do you think so many women become nuns?

"When I cut it short you said I looked like a punk."

"Admit it, you were going to hang out at seedy coffee shops and stop showering. You have an image to maintain."

"Please, for the love of god…"

"I do love you. "

"I know. You have to trust me. I am your one son made in your imagine. If you insult me aren't you insulting yourself."?

"I understand that but…what I'm saying is you need to stop wearing that halo. We get it, you're Jesus, but do you have to show off all the time. Maybe you could even try a new look, perhaps blue robes instead of white. As long as you don't wear black and look like a sixth lord any color works. There is so much potential. Oprah always wears very nice outfits"

"What if I wear a cape to show off my tough side?"

"Have you seen Oprah lately? Since she lost the weight she looks great. I'm a big fan."

Jesus decides things are getting out of hand and decides to cut to commercial.

"Well, I believe I am just as competent as Oprah, thank you. We'll be right back with our guest, god."

Upon further inquiry my teacher informs me a personal hero is someone who, through their bravery, makes you want to be a better person. She suggests using a family member, like a parent or grandparent. I love my parents with all my heart and they are great people but really, that is so lame. The first person I think of is my mom because she gave birth to me and with my antics I know I don't make it easy on her. When I think of a hero I think of someone or something swooping in with little regard for their own life, spitting in the face of danger, and doing whatever it takes to make things right. My hero rides a motorcycle and knows how to handle a weapon if necessary. My mom would never ride a motorcycle and hates guns. I have never seen her saving lives or kicking ass. All I can think of is my mom's strange characteristics. She has a very addictive personality. She is addicted to salt. As a kid she kept a saltshaker next to her bed in case she had a craving in the middle of the night. That's crazy. Every time my mom goes to the ocean she swallows the seawater just to get the salt. At that point you know you have a problem.

One year for Christmas my sister and I bought her a salt lick and put in under the Christmas tree as a joke. All I know is that when I woke up in the morning some of it was missing. My mom is also addicted to gum and coffee. She made me go into Starbucks almost every day because she was embarrassed that she went so much and they knew her by name. My mom also can't handle her liqueur which is probably a good thing but every time she has a little too many I think about her story of when she got drunk when she was thirteen. Apparently it was quite the big deal when it happened. She was a waitress at a fancy dinner party her parents were having. Some of the higher ups in the city were there, including city officials and wealthy benefactors. Every time a drink came back to the kitchen my mom chugged it down and got increasingly drunk as the night went on. My grandmother knew something was up when my mom was slurring her speech and spilled wine all over an aid to the mayor. It ended when my mom brought the cake out and as she placed it down on to the table passed out into it. My mom never drank much after that. She was too afraid she would have one beer and make a fool out of herself.

She does like to sing on the rare occasion that she drinks but in these cases I think she drinks just to have an excuse to sing in public. Not to mention my mom has some strange fears. When she was five she fell in a fishpond and the fish gathered around her. My mom says all she remembers is starring up and seeing a dense layer of fish sliding over her eyeballs. They were slimy and swimming all over her. In that moment she thought they would eat her whole and that would be the end of her. To this day she is deathly afraid of fish. I remember it used to be so bad, when I was a kid when the family went out to a restaurant no one was allowed to order fish.

She still swims in the lake from time to time but she is extra cautious. She looks around constantly and she immediately gets out at any sign of movement. One ripple and she is gone. Despite my mom's craziness, a week after the assignment is given I am still thinking about using her as my hero. I mean, she has always given me strong encouragement and had a big part in how I am today. She deserves a lot of credit for that and, despite her craziness, she is a good parent. I decide the paper will be about he and am prepared to write it. Then, as if on schedule, there is an incident that sends my entire family to the emergency room that my mom helps perpetuate. In the heat of the moment she panics and chaos ensues.

It all started with a honeybee. I used to be big fan of bees. They truly are remarkable creatures. For one, I love honey. You drizzle it on your toast in the morning and you have a delightful snack that will energize you for the rest of the day. Honey can literally be put on any food in my mind and it instantly makes it better. You can put it in tea, on hot cereals like oatmeal, drizzle it on waffles, and it goes great with both chocolate and peanut butter. The possibilities are endless. I also figure if a bear is attacking me I can throw honey at it and it will be so grateful it will become docile and cuddly. Winnie the Pooh loves honey and he is very cute and friendly. Of course, he and his gang of animal friends also taught me tigers can bounce high on their tails and are goofy. They are the unemployed clown of the animal kingdom.

When I went to the zoo as a kid I was confused why the tiger didn't talk and goof off. It just sat there and I kept harassing it to tell a joke it growled at me. I also thought donkeys were constantly depressed. Until the incident, I always wanted to do the thing where you cover yourself in bees. I saw this guy on T.V. do it once and it looked so cool. Who doesn't want a beard of bees? It would freak people out and I could claim I was a sorcerer. I would wear a long cloak of bees and release the hoard onto my victims when provoked. I would have so much power.

Most people don't know this, but the United States Government is even using bees in combat zones. A program was just started to use them to detect landmines. They train bees to cluster over spots where the landmine is buried. There are current efforts to see if they can equip bees with powerful lasers so when the bees cluster over a landmine a laser attached to the bees abdomen will diffuse it. It sounds crazy but animals' packing high-powered lasers is a genius idea. Imagine a woman walking alone down a dark alley. You can hear the clack of her shoes hitting the pavement and see her shadow dancing on the wall. Behind her another appears, menacing and ominous in the darkness. She instinctively clutches her purse close to her chest and starts to walk faster. The shadow gets closer and the woman cowers in fear because she knows no one is around to hear her scream. Suddenly, out of nowhere, appears a rhinoceros with a laser strapped to it. It would scare the crap out of potential criminals. Knowing there are large animals strapped with lasers roaming the streets, criminals wouldn't go out at night and crime would be drastically reduced. You wouldn't even have to pay the animals. Other scary animals could be used too: like lions, deranged monkeys, penguins in the winter, and sharks patrolling the oceans for pirates. Of course, if the animals become unruly you have a real problem. Aggressive beasts running around the streets firing lasers at people is never good.

The prelude to the larger bee incident happened one day in late summer outside the rental house my family was staying in while our house in the woods was being built. It was a sunny day and on days like this I got up early when there was still a thin layer of dew on the grass. It was so freeing to run around outside barefoot. Once I did it naked and my mom got many complaints from the neighbors. It's funny how older adults seeing you naked is viewed so differently depending on your age. If you are very young it is cute. If you are a teenager it is embarrassing and never to be discussed again. If you are a young adult it is awkward and there is the inevitable conversation about sex and being proud of your body. If you are middle aged it is at first shockingly horrifying and then becomes funny if they got a good look. They might also view it as a cry for help.

If the man is insecure they might ask everyone that has seen them naked to verify it isn't that bad. If the parent is old enough to see you naked as an old man then it is written of as a momentary lapse of reason or the signs of being senile. Luckily, on this particular day I was completely clothed except my feet. I started to walk past the side of my house through a particularly large section of overgrown grass. As I walked grasshoppers sprang up all over the place, creating a green blizzard of insects. I used to run through this area and pretend I was a giant. The grasshoppers were the lowly humans on the ground trying to take me down with missiles, assault rifles, and grenades.

Suddenly I felt a sharp pain in my foot. I try to take a step but a sharper pain expands over my entire foot and I fall to the ground. The grasshoppers swarm me, sensing a perfect time to strike. I limp into the house. It turns out I have stepped on a bee and the stinger has lodged into my foot. The pain has shot up my leg and my foot has swelled. Half an hour later I am in the hospital waiting room. I recall all the other times I have been here. There was the time I shoved a cooked carrot up my nose and it had to be extracted with long tweezers. I believe I was a curious kid and wondered if I could taste it with my nose. The logic went against everything I knew about how the nose functioned but I had to find out. It's possible I was going to eat it but simply missed my mouth. The orange color of the carrot should have been seen as a caution sign that I should stop but I ignored it. No color was going to tell me what to do. Oddly enough, after the carrot incident orange became my favorite color.

As I wait to get my foot looked at I look around the waiting room and am trying to figure out what they are in for. One lady has her hat shoved down over her eyes. Either she has committed a crime and hopes no one will notice her or her hat is glued to her head. Another guy has a red swollen eye. He could have been hit or he works for a traveling sideshow. His trick is he can take his eye out of its socket and put it back in. That would be an awesome trick. You could do that if you had a glass eye and really wanted to freak out your friends. I imagine people in the park playing marbles and the glass eye being used to knock little marbles out of the circle. It would be crazy if three different people with glass eyes took them out and then you juggle them and do magic tricks with them. I would pay to see that show. It would be really crazy if the three people got confused and the glass eyes ended up in different people's sockets. All I need to do is find three people with glass eyes and we could make money as a traveling show or as street performers.

The woman sitting in the corner really fascinates me. She is dressed in a flashy red gown with matching handbag. She must have come from some fancy party. She is holding her wrist gingerly in her hand and moving it around to test the ligaments. I notice her dress is singed with black down one side and the red high heel on her left foot is blackened and melted. The foot looks smashed and swollen. What could possibly have happened? She must have been juggling fire when she missed a pin and it fell on her foot. If this were the case the thing she was juggling would have to be very heavy. Maybe it was a flaming bowling ball. I got it. She was juggling three different objects. One was a bowling ball and one was a flaming pin. She threw the bowling ball so high it hurt her wrist so she dropped it on her foot. The pain distracted her and she dropped the flaming pin. It traveled down the side of her dress and fell onto the same foot causing the plastic shoe to melt and blacken. I give a little fist pump in my chair. Wow, I am a regular Sherlock Holmes. My cunning expertise and attention to detail is unrivaled and I succeed in solving the toughest medical mysteries.

After a long wait I am finally called to a smaller waiting room. I am told the doctor will be right with me. When I get older I hate this part because they ask you to get undressed and change into a gown. I never know if I should get completely naked or not.

If I don't the doctor might ask me to do so before he sees me and then I have to wait even longer. About a year ago I slammed my foot into a door. I told the doctor I was worried I had broken a toe and he told me to change into a gown and he would be right back. Do I really have to get naked to have my foot looked at? I think it is more appropriate to roll up my pant legs than take them off. I also hate that the gowns tie in the back so I can't reach them by myself. Where is the attractive nurse to do it for you? It is too loose for comfort and I am letting everything hang out. It is humiliating. Then you have to sit there naked for an hour until the doctor returns.

It also bothers me that there is never anything to read in the smaller waiting room. I always get bored. I play with all the instruments and test them out to see if they work. I test the thermometers to see what my temperature is. I put a cold compress on my head while I am getting my temperature to see if this will have an effect. I test my blood pressure and wonder what the numbers actually mean. I lick all the tongue depressors and put them back. I have to do something to pass the time. When the doctor finally returns, he informs me I am allergic to bees and this is what caused my foot to swell up. He gives me an EpiPen. It is basically a needle that you jab yourself with when you get stung. The medicine in the syringe is meant to relieve the swelling. I guess my dream of having a beard of bees and having them attack on my command will no longer happen. I'm sad.

I don't have to use the EpiPen until about a year later. We are finally out of the rental house and I am no longer battling grasshoppers. We have officially moved in to the permanent residence in the woods. The house is very nice and the scenery is beautiful. The best part is the lake is within walking distance and there is a community dock we can use. To celebrate the move we invite family friends over for a barbeque and swimming. They have a son my age and a younger girl that is only a few years younger than my sister. My sister and I are standing on some old railway planks that mark the edge of the driveway. As their car is driving up the driveway the planks loosen and bees swarm from underneath. In a few seconds they are everywhere.

My mom and dad flee back inside the house as fast as they can. My sister falls and the bees engulf her. They fly up her shirt and she receives half a dozen stings before it's over. Meanwhile, before I can react I am stung on my upper arm, twice on my thigh, and the back of my neck. My sister and I run inside the house and to our dismay the bees follow close behind in hot pursuit. Some of them get inside and everyone is freaking out. My dad grabs a rolled up newspaper and starts swatting the bees out of the air. My sister is clutching at her back where most of the stings are. She collapses on the couch.

"Can someone get me some ice", she yells at no one in particular, "Hello, I'm in pain!"

The only one listening is my father and he is busy dismissing away angry bee attacks with expertly timed swats. It may be his years of playing tennis but he was made for this. He is keeping track of how many bees he kills and yells out the score after every one."

"Newspaper six, bees zero."

He looks heroic with a wide stance and the newspaper high up in the air behind his back. He looks like a baseball player in the fight of his life. With all the pain and chaos swirling around him, he loves this.

"Dad, forget the stupid bees. I need some ice."

"Hold on, just one more bee. The damn things keep coming."

"Dad…"

"Newspaper nine, bee zer…ow, wow that hurts…bee one."

Dad pauses with the newspaper high in the air

"Alright you stupid bees, it is on. Let's rumble"

"Dad!"

Meanwhile, I plop down in a chair in the living room. My mom runs to get the EpiPen and comes flying back. She is in a panic.

"What do I do?"

My mom is red and flustered. She looks around to see my dad running to the kitchen still waving the newspaper wildly and my sister face down on the couch. She looks woozy and her legs seem to buckle slightly. I need to get her attention back.

"Mom…"

"What? Oh, right. Can someone else do this?"

I look over to see my dad trip and spill ice all over the floor. He curses loudly and runs back to the kitchen for more. When he comes back in he slips on the wet floor, his feet flying out from under him. I hear the smack of his back hitting the floor.

"Relax mom, just jab me in the thigh and press the plunger."

She turns it over to look for directions but doesn't see any. It looks like a miniaturized rocket ship or a specialized number

2 pencil. It is yellow with a white round circle on one end and a clear plastic cylinder on the other.

"Where is the needle? Both ends look the same!"

I don't think I want her to do it now. She is shaking and the EpiPen is wavering back and forth. I look to see who else could possibly do it. My sister is lying on her stomach on the sofa in obvious pain, still waiting for ice. My dad has finally gotten up and is scooping up the fallen ice into a bucket cursing.

"Mom, you need to calm down. Relax and do it."

I close my eyes. I can't watch. I can imagine her missing and somehow managing to jab me in the eye. I cringe at the thought.

"No, wait. I am supposed to jab you in the thigh but do I have to hit a vain?"

"I'm in a lot of pain here."

My mom wipes sweat off her forehead. She is shaking. She closes her eyes and a calm comes over her.

"Okay, okay...it's okay...here we go."

My mom jabs The Epipen onto my thigh as hard as she can. There is a split second pause before she lets out a bloodcurdling scream.

"Ahhhhh..."

She has chosen the wrong end and stabbed herself in the thumb instead. My mom jumps up and starts waving her hand around. Upon hearing the noise my dad drops the ice he was carrying to bring to my sister.

"Oh come on. Will I ever get some damn ice?"

My mom is starting to feel woozy from what she has injected herself with and falls backwards onto the chair landing right in my lap. My dad has to drive all three of us to the emergency room. It feels like the car ride takes forever. My sister is sprawled out in the back seat with her eyes closed with ice packs all over her. She is moaning about something but I can't understand what she is saying. Between the incoherent moaning she is screaming about how she hates bees and they all should die. My mom is holding her thumb gently. It is bright red and swollen. Her head is swimming from the injection and it is bobbing back and forth. I'm not sure if she knows where she is or what has happened. As for me, I have some slight swelling but I'm a lot better off than my mom and sister. My dad is driving and talking to himself.

"How could she not know what end the needle is…how could she do that?"

Despite my moms state she is able to mumble a reply

"It was confusing. Can't you be more supportive? This hurts like crazy."

"I mean, it's a needle for goodness sake. One end has a sharp pointed end of shiny metal and the other does not. How is that complicated? It's just…"

"I had no time to think."

"It's not hard to figure out."

My mom screams at no one in particular.

"Damn it, I hate ****ing bees."

It feels like we hit every red light on the way to the hospital. Every so often my mom drifts off and I slap her in the face to keep her from going to sleep. I figure it is better to keep her awake. She is beyond loopy at this point and keeps mumbling about gumdrops and how she thinks she's a bee. We are all assuming it's the medicine but who knows. When we finally arrive at the hospital, we have to grad mom around the shoulders steer her through the front entrance. My sister is holding her back. My mom is admitted right away. She is put on a gurney this time spouting something about Smurfs and questioning why they are blue. My sister is admitted soon afterwards. I am the last one to get called. Finally the doctor I know all too well comes out with his clipboard.

"Nick, nice to see you again."

"Dr. Stenwick. This will be the last time, I swear."

I first saw him when I was young and shoved a cooked carrot up my nose. I saw him a week later when I remained curious and graduated to crayons. I saw him several years later when I got stitches on my chin and again when I first entered school and twisted my ankle getting into the bathtub. In fifth grade I burned my hand on the stove and in sixth grade I fell into a clothing rack and got a black eye. Of course that was pretty badass and I told the girls in my class I got in a fight with a kid much older and bigger than me and kicked his ass. He always told me I was his favorite patient and he would see me in a couple of years. It turns out I am fine but I receive a new Epipen just in case.

My sister receives treatment and is released later in the day with the areas of her stings patched and soothing ointment. My mom is given fluids to flush out her system and the swelling is treated. She is also released that day. Man, what a crazy day. That night I can't sleep and I start to rethink what a hero means to me and realize my mom really could be my hero. Yes, she may be absent minded sometimes and she did stab herself in the thumb, but she will always be there no matter what happens. She has helped shape who I am, having a strong influence on my morals and what I personally believe in. A week later I present Mr. Peanut as my personal hero, but at the end cite my mother as a close second.

COLLEGE

THE GOATS ARE ON THE FIELD

The University has a new president, Dr. Mary Shannon. She seems very nice and I am enthusiastic about changes she can make. The previous president, Dr. Alex Leroy, hated me because he doesn't understand how far I will go for an amazing prank. I think my first idea that pranks could be fun came from a colorful children's fable called "The Bad Kangaroo." my grandfather read to me on a trip to the lake. My parents actually recorded it and I listen to it every time I want to remember how much fun my grandfather was and how much he loved life. The story is about a family of lovable kangaroos. The son kangaroo goes to school with other young animals. There is a sassy young hippo, a curious young lion, a young giraffe that always gets picked on for being different, and the ditzy young flamingo that desperately wants to be a ballerina just to name a few. The teacher is an older uptight penguin.

The young son kangaroo is a mischievous and disruptive student in school and gets the other animals to act up too. He puts tacks on the teacher's chair and throws spitballs in class. He sets off firecrackers in the school bathroom and super glues the teacher's coffee cup to her desk. The penguin teacher waves her flippers in frustration and goes into hysterics when a spitball hits her in the face. Maybe this is why I misbehaved so much in Mr. Shank's class in elementary school. When the teacher is invited to dinner at the kangaroo family home to discuss the young kangaroos behavior things quickly get out of hand. The trouble starts when the teacher sits on a tack that has been placed on her chair by Mr. kangaroo. Mrs. Kangaroo throws a spitball at the teacher and when a loud bang is heard it is explained that the children are playing with firecrackers.

The teacher is forced to flee. She grabs the doorknob only to discover her hand has now been super glued to it. The message is something about children taking after their parents, much to the detriment of the children. I don't know if my parents liked to do pranks in school but it would make a lot of sense. Listening to the tape my grandfather is laughing so hard he can barely get through the story and as the tape continues he laughs for several minutes after it is finished. The tape ends with a loud crash of a lamp being knocked over and screams that the rug could catch on fire. It is my aha moment that I want to be like the young kangaroo and someday up the ante, doing creative pranks that people will never forget. Even as a kid I look to college as the place to do it.

When I first come to college I am scared and nervous to be completely on my own for the first time. I remember standing outside my dormitory the first day of classes and watching a group of friends sitting under a big oak tree laughing. I want the same thing but am nervous about approaching people I don't know. Suddenly out of nowhere a Frisbee hits me in the back of the head. A guy wearing aviator glasses runs over and invites me to play. His name is Ramon and he will become a major part of my college experience.

The adventures we get in to are grand and he inspires me to perform pranks around campus. With his guidance we go around playing jokes on students in my hallway before I decide they are so much fun and I break out on my own. Ramon will become very important to me later as the man that can get everything. My first pranks are pretty standard. A week after school starts I go into the freshman dorms and turn over all the furniture. I place helium balloons all over the lobby until the room is completely full. Students love it and even staff members are amused by it. Each student takes a balloon back to their room making clean up a breeze I've heard it said that my fun loving prank led to fewer disciplinary incidents in the dorms during traditionally the worst week. I am hooked.

After the young kangaroo, my new hero immediately becomes Marcus Wymer. He is the only person to get expelled from both Harvard and Yale, wreaking his havoc in the early 1920's. He was the first great prankster of our generation and if there were a prankster hall of fame he would get his own shrine. He got expelled from Yale for toilet papering millionaire J.P Morgan's yacht. He rented a private plane just to do it and made sure he picked a time that no one would notice. He planned the prank for days, securing blue prints of the boat and knowing exactly when the boat docks would be clear.

Marcus spent more time on the prank than classes but the man had a gift and he wasn't afraid to utilize his talents. Despite buying all the toilet paper from several local stores, Marcus was never caught and news of what happened spread quickly. I have to admit in homage of sorts I once got a group together and we toilet papered some friends cars. They banded together and what is commonly referred to by those involved as "The Night of Mayhem" was officially underway. Things got out of hand real quick. The night ended with lots of water balloons exploded and flour dumped all over everyone. Unfortunately our band of misfits lost the battle. I was heavily flowered and our leader got duck tapped to a pole. It was pretty humiliating.

Word about "Night of Mayhem" spread across campus and all the freshman dorms were excited to participate. Prank Wars was born. The plan was to have all the freshman dorms engage in a night of pranks until one dorm emerged victorious. Prank Wars became a tradition that is now done the first day of Homecoming Week every year. I had a small part in forever changing the campus climate and it wouldn't be the last time either. If toilet papering the boat wasn't enough Marcus also got drunk during a theatre production on campus and threw a beer bottle at the stage cursing and mocking one of the professors in attendance.

"I am Henry Hallam Tweedy, professor of Homiletics at the Harvard Divinity School. I am a moron."

After getting expelled from Yale Marcus went to Harvard. I'm not sure how he got admitted with his reputation but he deserved entrance simply based on his genius as a mischief-maker. A week into his first year he was somehow about to get a limited edition model T Ford car on to the roof of the commons building in the middle of campus. No one could figure out how the prank had been pulled off and how the car had gotten up there. Students, Faculty, and Administration were stunned. They had never seen anything like this before and word quickly spread about the unbelievable act. Newspapers from around the country came to document the event. Many of the students believed it was pure magic and school officials even questioned several local magicians. In a related story, one gullible student became so convinced magic was real that he thought legendary magician Harry Houdini was invincible and could not be hurt. The student met Houdini backstage after a show and punched him hard in the stomach. Ironically Harry Houdini could escape straightjackets, locked water tanks, and buried caskets but a punch to the stomach took his life.

The prank was soon dubbed the case of the magic car. It caused a huge sensation across the country and became legendary. The depression was in full swing. In an era dominated by news about the economy it was the headline story in newspapers including The New York Times and The Boston Globe. When school administrators finally figured out who had pulled off the act they marveled at Marcus's genius but still had no choice but to expel him. Just thinking about how much planning and preparation went into the stunt I can't help but be impressed. To this day no one is certain how the great feat and arguably the greatest prank of all time, was pulled off. There are theories such as the use of an industrial sized crane or the art of Voodoo but the mystery still remains. That man is a genius and took pranks to a whole new level.

Before the previous president left I decided I had to pull off the perfect prank, one that would go down in University lore. I think back to my days in high school and the crazy things I used to do. When I first started doing pranks I did juvenile things like putting rice in my dad's umbrella. When he went outside and opened it up the rice rained down upon him. I thought it was hysterical but he wasn't as amused. A friend of mine has a ceiling fan. One day I took Styrofoam cups filled with confetti and taped them to the top of the fan blades. When he turned it on soon after, confetti went everywhere. It was pretty awesome until I realized I had to clean it up.

The best prank I pulled was against my cranky neighbor who would sit on his porch and angrily stare at all the neighbors going past walking their dogs. If a dog even put one paw onto his lawn he would yell and scream and say he was calling the cops. I knew I had to do something that would get him back for all problems he caused and hopefully even make him laugh. I snuck into his house one day, not an easy feat, and filled all his cabinets with ping-pong balls. When the cranky man came home and opened his cabinet they showered down all over his head. Several cabinets later and ping-pong balls fill the small kitchen. I didn't hear anything about what he thought about the prank but I assume he loved it. Eventually the pranks of my youth become stale and I decide to put them on hold until college.

Within a month of entering school I once again become excited about doing pranks. I carry around a notebook chock full of creative ideas. Between the family of mischievous kangaroos and Marcus Wymer I have to be careful. Marcus created a ruckus but never caused anyone any harm. The best prank has to be good natured and humorous or it just isn't very fun. It's also important it remains anonymous and I do not get caught. The timing of the prank is also very important. I want to pick a time that will get the most attention. My first idea is to do it during homecoming week where there will be plenty of school officials and alumni present. I thought maybe I could do it during the parade and build a really inappropriate float featuring two gigantic paper mache figures in sexually compromising positions. Two people would run along the float dressed as a vagina and a penis singing and dancing to Barbara Streisand songs.

I have the mental image of two oversized costumes with tiny white clad legs sticking out. They could bump into each other suggestively but that might be taking it too far. Instead of candy I would throw out condoms attached to lollipop sticks into the crowd. It would be an educational opportunity to promote safe sex. With all the children in attendance there would be some pretty upset parents. Truth be told, if I saw this display I might even be offended. Seeing a giant penis with little white arms and legs sticking out running around the streets would just be wrong. After I scrap the idea I have nightmares about it. I dream people dressed as giant penises are chasing me but no matter how fast I run they get closer and closer. They are multiplying before my eyes and now there is a large mass of them. It is like a scene in a movie where villagers with pitchforks and torches chase down the monster terrorizing their village. They come at me from all sides and corner me against a brick wall. There is no way out. I wake up in a cold sweat.

I pass the float idea by my roommate Edward but he just stares at me. He's highly religious and he doesn't want to have sex until he is married. I totally respect that but I think he takes it too far. Edward found a girlfriend that compliments his ideals through an online Christian dating site. She comes to visit every weekend and I dread it every time. When she comes to visit he will not allow her to sleep in his bed or even in the same room I guess to resist the temptation. Unfortunately this means she takes the bed and Edward sleeps on the couch in the Resident Hall lobby. I must tell you this makes me extremely uncomfortable. I lie in bed trying to sleep while she drones on about her life. I want to care that she feels her cat Whiskers is ignoring her but I have no idea what to say. I am not a cat psychologist.

When she starts crying I try and comfort her by saying maybe the cat just needs some extra attention and giving it catnip certainly doesn't hurt. She accuses me of trying to drug her cat and calls me immoral. She also always asks me about sex. She wants to know what it feels like and she has so many misconceptions. She asks why men always cry afterwards and asserts that to her it's not a big deal because after you have a kid you can't have sex anymore. I try to reassure her to the contrary and say this is a conversation she should have with

Edward. I try to end the conversation but she keeps talking. She has so many questions and wants to know how I could be so sinful. As her speech becomes faster and increases in intensity I'm pretty sure I start to scream in horror and soon pass out from too much sensory overload.

I quickly discard the float idea and realize I need to keep the prank relatively simple and ultimately harmless. After classes are over for the day I walk around campus and study every building and every outside area. The place where the prank will take place is extremely important. I scribble notes in my notebook. The library is a possibility. Lots of books and a quiet atmosphere waiting to be disrupted could be a possibly perfect place. I also learn everything I can about major players on campus including administration and staff. I have to know how they would react in a prank situation and how quickly it would take them to act. Late one night, with all the information collected and after much planning, I decide upon the ultimate prank involving three separate incidents. I gather all the supplies I need but the hardest thing to ascertain.

I need three goats. You may ask why I chose goats but in reality it makes so much sense. When I was a kid I watched a cartoon featuring a talking goat named Billy Goat Gruff. He looked harmless enough eating tin cans and minding his own business but that was the key. His perceived harmlessness was deceiving. He guarded a bridge and wouldn't let anyone pass unless they solved a riddle. I remember it being able to breath fire and I think it ate the people that couldn't get the riddle correct. The show didn't really make much sense. At one point the goat went back in time and the show lost all credibility. I chose goats for several reasons. Goats have the coolest beards of any animal. Goat beards are long, white, and wispy like an old wizard's. I imagine the goat deep in thought stroking its beard inquisically. Most importantly even the females have beards and that's just cool. Secondly, goats are known to eat anything and that is perfect for what I am trying to accomplish. Hopefully I get some really hungry goats. In addition, no one would suspect a goat. I'm not really sure what they do all day besides be weird looking and eat everything in sight.

I know I need goats but am unsure where to get them. I turn to my friend Ramon for help. He is known on campus as the guy who can get anything. He has short brown choppy hair and sports a well-groomed goatee. Add in Aviator glasses and a black leather jacket and he looks like a badass. He rides a motorcycle and the ladies dig it. He has a don't care attitude that is infectious and people gravitate towards him. Every time I talk to him I get flustered and wonder if I am being as cool as him.

Seeing how popular he was I once tried to emulate his charm. One day I wore all black and drove his motorcycle around but didn't get any attention. One of the elderly librarians whistled at me but she was the only one that seemed to notice. I now know it is possible to whistle even if you are missing most of your teeth. I assume it is the goatee. He looks like a well-groomed Hispanic soap opera star. I try to grow a beard but it always ends up weird and patchy. Needless to say Ramon is the big man on campus and everyone knows who he is. He is known as the man who can make it happen. A fraternity was having a Hawaiian themed party on campus and requested sand and a real palm tree. I have no idea how Ramon did it but people made sand castles and relaxed in the shade of several palm trees. Others drank Caribbean martinis and sunbathed by the pool.

I did request another animal once. I had just watched the historical Epic "Ben Hur" and was quite intrigued. I wanted to have a horse pull me in a chariot around campus. I of course would be donned in full armor and carrying a whip. I figure if someone challenges me to a fight I will be prepared. Ramon gets me the horse but can't get the chariot. I have the horse pull me in a golf cart instead. As I travel down the main street on campus crowds gather on both sides wondering what in the world is going on. I feel on top of the world. I, of course, have a bullhorn with me. I emit battle cries and challenge passers by to epic sword fights. I imagine I am Russell Crowe from the movie gladiator and must fight trained soldiers and man-eating tigers to earn my release. The fairest lady in the kingdom, of course, falls in love with me. I must look regal until the horse bucks and my golf cart veers into a parked car. I fly from the golf cart and fall over the roof of the car and onto the ground. The car alarm blares and the horse gallops off. I get to my feet and run wildly after it while on lookers stare after me. Man, what a rush. After the stunt I walk in to the campus bookstore donned in full gleaming armor to get a soda but no one seems to notice. Afterwards I talk to campus police.

"Son, what were you thinking?

"I am honoring Roman history which I am studying in Mr. Bell's history class. The golf cart clearly represents a chariot. What can I say; I think higher education means learning inside and outside of the classroom. I hope to receive extra credit."

I receive a citation and a fine but it was totally worth it. I had a friend video tape it and put it on YouTube. It has currently gotten one million hits and I am somewhat of an Internet celebrity. With the idea fully planned out I approach Ramon about getting the goats. He simply smiles.

"You son of a bitch. You must be planning something crazy."

"Well..."

58

The first part of my plan runs smoothly. My speech teacher, Dr. Walker, is someone I have always wanted to prank. She is so nice to all her students and loves when I act up a little in class. She smiles and trying to hide her amusement she wags a finger at me. I've discussed prank ideas with her before and for a prank of this magnitude she would want to be the first recipient. She is very thin with thin arms that seem to extend down past her knees. Her legs are long and she has very narrow feet that cause her to sway from side to side when she walks. What makes matters worse is that she hunches over when she talks and has a low guttural voice. It is husky in tone and I imagine it would be considered quite alluring in her younger days. On the morning of the prank Dr. Walker wakes up early and prepares for her morning class. Needing a pick me up she heads to the dining hall and grabs a quick cup of coffee. She particularly loves Brazilian Roast Nut coffee because she assumes it tastes exotic. In reality its just regular coffee falsely labeled and served in a fancy cup.

She walks to her office across campus. I'd like to imagine she is skipping happily and whistling her favorite tune. She is in a great mood. She opens her office door and flicks on the lights to see a goat eating the papers on her desk. She jumps back with a start and the goat looks up from the desk. Dr. Walker lets out a low guttural scream and the goat goes crazy. It starts kicking its legs and running wildly around the office. Dr. Walker runs from her office and doesn't stop screaming until she has exited the building. Students walking outside stare on and many laugh as she tries to calm herself down. The goat meanwhile remains in her office the rest of the day just chilling out and snacking on some fruit left over from the lunch Dr. Walker had a day previously. In reality goats are very mild mannered. They may freak out from time to time when confined to such a small space but all they really want is a good meal. I admire them really. They are very cultured, not afraid to eat anything that looks remotely edible.

Reportedly, Dr. Walker became deathly afraid of goats. She says they are aggressive and devilish creatures. She refuses to drive through any farmland so she won't see any wandering around. At any sound that sounds remotely like a 'bahhhhh' or a 'mehhh' she scrunches up her nose and bolts in the other direction. She demanded that one of her speech students shave his wispy gray beard because it was giving her traumatic flashbacks. After several weeks of showing her pictures of goats harmlessly eating grass and reassuring her they are not out to get her, she was fine. The administration set up a "Goat Taskforce" to investigate the situation but nothing was discovered and it was concluded to be an isolated incident. They were wrong.

With the first part of my plan accomplished perfectly I move on to step two of my prank. For phase two I needed the perfect environment and the perfect person. I needed someone who would take the incident seriously but have no clue how to handle it. I know the perfect person. Ronald Moore is someone I have always wanted to prank. He would be a distinctive figure in an endless sea of morons and I suspect he is a little crazy. His reaction to a prank would be priceless. Ron is director of the Student Union building, located directly in the middle of campus. It is where students hang out. There is an eating area, bowling and billiards, and a student lounge with a TV.

My favorite Ron story happened at a Student Union meeting with the entire Student Affairs staff present. His immediate boss is the leader of the meeting, Beth, and on rare occasions the president of the University herself is present. There is an eating area outside the Student Union building with a grill and tables with umbrellas. I have never seen a student actually go out there and I doubt anyone even knows it is there. The trashcan outside in the area lasts a good five years and costs a mere $100 to replace. In his infinite wisdom Ron decided to buy a $3,000 stainless steel trashcan because it would never have to be replaced and is more durable. With the economy on the slide state funding is limited and the budget is heavily scrutinized. A poor purchase could have devastating results on the school's future funding. Ron brought up his purchase at a budget meeting of all places. Beth, the director of Student Affairs and the leader of the meeting, is about to end the meeting when Ron raises his hand with a smile.

"Yes, I have purchased something for the Student Union that I am very proud about"

Beth frowns and stares at Ron.

"I'm sure it can wait"

"No, this is very important. This will help make everything run more smoothly."

"If this has anything to do with another pirate outfit for you to wear I will be upset. And for the last time, Timmy the squirrel does not need an outfit to keep it warm in the winter."

Ron is about to open his mouth to protest but based on the scowl directed his way decides against it. In truth Ron loves that squirrel. Every night he leaves cut up chicken outside on the patio behind the Student Union building. Ron gets confused when it remains uneaten. People try and explain to him squirrels eat nuts and not meat but it doesn't seem to work.

"But…"

"Alright, what is it this time?"

"I bought a trashcan for the Student Union. It will never rust or have to be replaced."

"Well, I do remind you that because of the complete magic set you bought yourself with student funds you must get my permission to buy things. This; However, seems like a sound purchase. You have finally showed you can be responsible with a budget. I am very proud of you. How much did it cost?"

Ronald Moore beams from ear to ear. This is his moment to shine, the perfect opportunity for Ron to impress his colleagues. He pauses for dramatic effect and clears his throat.

"A mere 3,000 dollars."

Beth raises her eyebrows

"Okay, this better be a joke."

"Uh…"

"What, is it encrusted in diamonds?"

"I don't think so…"

"For goodness sake, I was being sarcastic. You do know…I can't believe…How many times have I told you to be careful with the budget?"

Ron hangs his head and looks like a sad little puppy. He can't believe it.

"But I have made some good purchases. What about those fake trees I bought? It really adds to the atmosphere of the building."

"A couple perhaps but you bought hundreds of them. It is like a damn jungle in this place. I can't even go to the bathroom because there are trees taking up all the space. Why in the world is there so many in the woman's bathroom and not the men's."

Don looks around with a disappointed frown. The look is reminiscent of a child who has just had a cookie slapped out of his hand.

"I thought women liked foliage?"

Everyone in the room shifts uncomfortably in their seat and looks at Beth in anticipation. There might be fireworks.

"Ron, that's…I really don't want to take away your purchasing abilities altogether, but…"

"What about the trashcan?"

"Put it in the outside area so no one can see it and question why we got it. I will deal with you after the meeting."

Everyone breathes out, knowing full well Ron has made a lot of poor purchases in the past and this is by far the worst. The purchase of the trashcan becomes known around the office and campus as Ron's folly. For a week after the meeting when Ron arrives in the morning a fake tree is placed outside his office door as a joke. The purchase of the trees is called Ron's folly 2. It is funny at first, but every time he sees the tree Ron bursts into tears and it soon becomes very sad. The bad purchases he has made are starting to add up. He bought a set of motorized scooters costing a total of $5,000. Ron claimed the scooters would save time getting around campus. For one, it is a small campus. It takes only five minutes to walk from one end to the other. Ron drove it around campus for pleasure. He even created a private parking space for it by blocking one off in front of the building with orange cones and caution tape. I admire the man though. To go out of your way to be that lazy is something I strive for. I dream big. On his birthday Ron hung piZatas all over the building and spent the entire day wandering around breaking them all open and eating the candy. The look of excitement on his face really made my day. He even paid a student to follow him around and make him balloon animals whenever he requested them. He is enthusiastic if nothing else.

Ron also spent institutional dollars on buying a full pirate outfit. It was complete with pirate hat and a $1,000 replica of a sword used in the 1800's off the coast of Spain in a sea faring battle. He wears the outfit around the office every Halloween. Don insists people call him Captain Bohel and talk like a pirate when addressing him. Last year he threatened the secretary with the sword claiming she was a murderous scallywag and should walk the plank. If I walk into his office next year to find a talking parrot I will really be freaked out. When the decision is made to keep him from making budgetary decisions Ron is crestfallen.

Maybe Ron is in the wrong job. He would make a great birthday party clown. Sure he can't juggle or do any magic tricks but he can be comical without even trying. He could make faces while trying to eat a piece of cake and all the kids would laugh. I have seen the man eat and he never seems to make his mouth on the first attempt. If he continues to struggle he claps his hands together and giggles. If Ron did earnestly try and eat cake he would probably get icing all over his face. He once walked around the Student Union building the entire day with easy cheese in his hair. No one had the heart to tell him. Ron could also make funny faces and pretend he was a mime. Hmmm, if you put him in an imaginary box, though, he would get confused and not know how to get out. I decide the Student Union building is the perfect setting for phase two of my prank and Don Bohel reacting to it will be the icing on the cake.

A week later the Student Union building is crowded with people eating lunch. People are enjoying their meals and listening to music from the University radio station. Happiness is in the air and I am just the man for the job to ruin it. I stand on the back patio where there is a grill and outdoor eating area. I see the black stainless steel trashcan Ron bought and smile. It really is just a trashcan and isn't even aesthetically pleasing. This is going to be great. I open the back door leading into the building, release the goat, and quickly run away. The goat runs around the room, eating burgers and sandwiches off people's plates. People get up in shock while others just sit there stupefied. Some people flee the room as if the goat were some enormous beast. Others gather on the sides of the room and watch the festivities. Ronald Moore runs into the room. He stops and sees the goat milling around the tables in the middle of the room. He eyes the goat suspiciously. Slowly but surely he quietly creeps up on the animal in an attempt to restrain it. Finally Ron has gotten behind the animal and opens his arms up wide to grab it. A murmur runs through the groups of students in the room. Suddenly the goat lets out a yelp and runs. Ron dives to the ground, cursing as he grabs only air on the way down. Getting up he smacks his head on the underside of a table. Students laugh as Ron rubs his poor bruised head and ego.

With a groan he runs around the room trying to catch the runaway goat. He curses loudly as people stare on in shocked silence and then slowly begin to laugh. It just makes Ron curse louder. Poor guy, he looks so confused. He resembles a hunchback zombie really, hunched over at the waist and running around in circles making low groaning noises and cursing. The goat finally stops running and begins eating hotdogs off a table next to the entrance to the café's kitchen. With a look of absolute focus on his face, Ron slowly sneaks up behind the animal for a second time. His shoes squeak on the floor and he freezes in place, holding his breath until his face turns red. The goat raises it's head and looks around for a brief second but the hotdogs are too tasty. The crowd watching the incident let out a gasp. Ron is so close to his goal his eyes glint in the light. Whether it's a sign of intense focus or insanity is up for debate. Ron now stands inches behind the goat. He raises his arms high above his head in preparation to pounce when the goat rears back his hind legs and kicks Ron flush in the groin. He doubles over and lets out a groan. He lies on the floor in the fetal position as the goat runs around him in circles. Everyone around him is laughing. While Ron is dealing with the goat I sneak into his office. He has a dry erase board next to his computer to remind him of what he needs to get done during the day. I write on the board: "Having fun with the goat? Wait until homecoming."

Ron immediately launches a full investigation. At first he thinks the mischievous goat wrote the message on his message board until someone explains to him it's not possible. Next, he organizes a "Goat Investigative Team" to investigate all leads that come into a special call center dubbed "Goat Central". Needless to say, he takes the incident very seriously. He even uses student funds to buy extensive goat outfits so his team can go undercover and find the real goat. Beth locks herself in her office the rest of the week and refuses to deal with it. Every day for the next week, Ron pulls students into his office, shines a light in their face, and grills them for information. At the end of his questioning, he always brings out a whip as an interrogation tactic. It doesn't scare anyone and inspires the school newspaper headline: "Ron Bowel: Tortures for pleasure and really into S & M." The investigation proves fruitless and Beth finally retains order and shuts it down. Nevertheless, tensions remain high with Homecoming fast approaching.

Several weeks later homecoming has finally arrived and it is a beautiful day. The sun is shining and there is no rain in the forecast. You can't ask for anything better on the day of homecoming. There are all the typical floats. A sorority sister dances on a float and throws out beads. I find it all pointless. If there are beads there should be some flashing involved. The float also features a limbo contest between all the sorority girls and is actually quite entertaining. A fraternity has a sports float featuring a goal post and a paper mache football. They are all dressed up in jerseys and helmets. The school's fight song is playing in the background. The Gamers and Anime Guild has a float featuring members dressed as wizards, hobbits, and dwarfs. I head down an alley next to the parade route and meet with Ramon. He is wearing a tan trench coat and a brown hat. He looks like he is about to whip out a Tommy gun and assassinate a mob informant. When I see him he looks around suspiciously. I half expect undercover informants to surround us and tell us to surrender our weapons.

I have always liked the idea of the Mafia. It is a tight nit family based on trust. It has your back no matter what happens. No one goes against the family. I want to be the town Godfather. I would have an accent just like in the movie. Townspeople would pay me to protect their turf. I would get free meals and complimentary merchandise everywhere I went. I would be respected and, of course, I would take care of my own. Realistically there is no way this would work. Sometimes I feel like the town is a hippy commune and no one has any money to pay. The only crime is someone stealing a roommate's indie C.D. or eating the last cracker. Ramon opens his jacket and pulls a set of keys out of the inside pocket. They glint in the sunlight and I can't help but smile. I had a basic idea of what would happen when I released the other two goats. This time I am unsure. In the end I decided three just wasn't enough. My final prank would require many more.

With a smile on my face I walk back up the parade route. Boring float after boring float slowly passes until one catches my eye. The float has beautiful women wearing long black skirts and white corsets under black tops. There are also figures dressed as skeletons. They all dance amongst each other to the sound of bongos. I wonder what group on campus would do this. There is the chess group and some of them are pretty smart but there is no way the guys in the group know that many beautiful women. It could be the fencing group but there are only 2 consistent members. Suddenly smoke billows from the center of the float and up through the myriad of beautiful maidens comes Ronald Moore in all his glory. I am stunned. He is donning the full pirate outfit he wears every Halloween and is hefting a large sword that looks way too big for him to carry. He also has a microphone, which is not good for anyone. I am very afraid of what he is going to say. He looks stoic albeit quite insane. To everyone's horror he starts to sing:

"A rollicking band of pirates we,
We seek revenge and sail the seven seas.
Raping and pillaging all the land that we may see,
We'll take your woman and your head despite your mighty plea."

With all the children in attendance this seems borderline inappropriate. While he is singing Ron starts dancing and making slashing motions in the air with the sword. On the other end of the float I see a woman who has been tied up. She struggles to get free as Ron Saunters over to her and places the sword against her cheek. He speaks into the microphone.

"Shiver me timbers. Arrrrg. Any last words before I make you walk the plank?"

She looks at the crowd with tears in her eyes

"Please, This man is crazy. Won't someone please save me?"

What is going on? I look at the far end of the float and sure enough there is a long plank of wood extended off of it. You have got to be joking me. I look around at the crowd. They look nervous and are looking around at each other for some sort of confirmation that everything is under control. Several kids next to me are crying. This could all be staged and there is really nothing to worry about. I'd like to assume that is the case but I can't tell. Ron starts to lead the crying woman towards the plank when out of no where a man wearing a black cape runs in and starts sword fighting with Ron screaming something about rescuing his one true love. It is really all too much for me to take and I have work to do. As I walk away I look over my shoulder to see Ron being impaled. He screams something about honor and falls to his knees. As I walk away I can hear him dying.

"You have slain me brave warrior. I spill my blood for you dear maiden and will die an honorable death but before I die I will kill everyone in the crowd."

I look over my shoulder for one last look to see a canon being brought to the center of the float. The crowd gasps and claps. What a great prop. There is a small wick on top of it and for a moment it doesn't register. Don puts down his sword and picks up a long match. Is he…there is no way. He dances around with the match. With a big grin on his face he strikes the match and the flame flares. He stares at it in excitement before he slowly brings the match down and lights the wick. Some of the people in the crowd are screaming and others are fleeing the street. Is this real? Regardless, he has finally lost his damn mind. As I watch the wick burn I can only imagine the aftermath: A building crumbling from the impact, Ron being dragged away in handcuffs yelling about how he will make them all walk the plank to be fed to the alligators. Poor Ron. Has it really come to this? Sure he is crazy, but he is a simple man with a good heart. I guess sometimes underneath a soft exterior lays an insane and rebellious mind that is just waiting to be let loose and wreak its havoc upon the world.

The wick has burned out. I cover my ears and crouch down to the pavement. A loud bang is heard and confetti sprays all over the crowd. I breathe out a sigh of relief. My heart is still pounding. I probably should have realized there was no way it could be a real cannon but with Ronald Moore I can never be sure. My greatest fear is that someday he will accidently blow up the Student Center or somehow manage to burn it to the ground. Last year he saw a bug in one of the bathrooms and wanted to spray the Student Center with deadly chemicals. Ron has not taken into account the smoke though.

It billows from the cannon and engulfs the float. The smoke is so thick the float has completely disappeared and the crowd around the float is coughing and covering their eyes. People run for cover in the confusion. When the smoke clears enough to see what is happening I see the float is out of control. It jumps the sidewalk and barrels through the crowd lining the streets. It finally smashes into a store front cracking a window and causing the store front awning to crash to the ground. Part of me wants to stay and see what happens in the aftermath, but I have work to do. It makes me happy knowing this will not be the craziest thing people see this faithful day.

Two hours later everything is set. The set of moving vans is in place and the new halftime announcement is ready to be read. The football game starts and I am getting nervous. It's actually a pretty good game with a lot of big plays. Our quarterback fires a bomb downfield and it is caught for a touchdown in the corner of the end zone. The score is tied when just before half time one of our corner backs jumps in front of a short slant rout and returns it the length of the field for a touchdown. The halftime show starts and the band takes the field. The PA system crackles and the sound of Ramon's voice booms over the field.

"Ladies and Gentlemen this is truly a grand day. For your halftime entertainment let me present our newest club on campus. I present to you in their debut performance; the dancing goats."

The gate on the outside of the field is opened and a herd of goats suddenly stampedes on to the field. There are about fifty in all. The marching band tries to flee but they might as well have been running in quick sand. Band members brace themselves as the herd crashes into the group. Instruments go flying in every direction as the sound of crashing metal and high-pitched screams can be heard reverberating through out the stadium. In the chaos band members are running in every direction at once, crashing into each other. They are doing more damage to each other than the goats are. Some of the goats have stopped and are trying to eat the band members clothing. They try to pull away but fall and the goats are pinning them down to keep eating. One goat manages to yank down the pants of one of the tuba players and he quickly runs from the field being chased by the goat. The goat tears his pants off and starts eating them. Apparently, they are pretty tasty. One goat seems to single out a specific band member and charges hard. As the goat bears down on her with his horns out she blocks the blow with her symbols. They bang horns to symbols several times, a ritual to win the heart of a woman goat. The crowd gasps and some clap. They are enjoying the show.

Eventually, the band members are able to run off and the goats just stand there milling about. They start eating the grass on the field. The athletic director and several people from the maintenance crew run onto the field screaming that the goats are trampling the grass. Do they not realize the goats are acting as a natural mower? The police have arrived and they run on to the field as the crowd boos. Unfortunately for them the goats have no problem being around people and do not react to the police. They clearly don't know how to herd animals. Each police officer grabs a goat and tries to drag it off the field. They are heavy and just stand there. They will not budge. The officers look at each other sheepishly and the crowd laughs.

The officers eventually band into a small group and decide they will force the goats off the field. They run at the goats from one side hoping they will be herded off the field but there are too many of them and they scatter in all directions. The crowd "ohhs" and "ahhs" with each failed attempt. After each failure there is much screaming and cursing from the officers. It is a great time.

As I sit inconspicuously in the stands, I laugh along with the rest of the crowd. I have pulled it off, in my mind a prank of mammoth proportions. I give thumbs up to the sky, hoping someplace; somewhere my hero Marcus Wymer has a big smile on his face. I can't even begin to describe to you the absolute thrill and rush of adrenaline I felt that day. Participants in extreme sports always talk about the thrill of adventure and I think I experienced something just as strong that day. Some people jump off cliffs or climb to the highest peek on earth but for the purest thrill there is nothing like watching careful planning and flawless execution result in the perfect prank. For a brief second I feel totally alive. The administration never found out it was me. They questioned Ramon because of his reputation but they had no evidence against him and he never gave me up. I figured someone would eventually match him to the voice heard over loud speaker but no one ever does. Every year since people have tried to pull off a grander prank but none of them have been successful and most of them get caught.

One thing I did not foresee is Ron's reaction to the prank. I figured he would be embarrassed. After the float fiasco he spent the night in jail for disturbing the peace and did not hear about the goats until the following morning when Beth used her own money to bail him out. When Beth told him what happened a slow devilish grin crept across his and she became

ADVENTURES IN AWKWARDNESS

even more outraged at him. I've heard that for years Ron has wanted to change the school's mascot. Our current mascot is a Ram named Stevenson. Several years ago Ron tried to pet it and he was rammed in the stomach at a football game. Then and there he vowed the mascot would be changed and for some reason it had to be an animal.

Two years ago he brought in a chicken named Elmer and said it would be the perfect mascot. He claimed it required hardly any upkeep and could be quite aggressive when cornered. People had to explain to him naming the sports teams "the chickens" was not a good idea. He protested that to make it more badass we could be the "fighting chickens." When this still didn't work he said it could be the "angry chickens" or even the "evil chickens." Ron would not be deterred though. Last year he brought in a python to be the new mascot but it got loose in the building. To this day it has not been found and Beth checks her office every morning to make sure it is not hiding out, ready to strike. When Ron would not stop and brought in a badger, followed by a baby crocodile, and finally a duck he was almost fired. Shortly after the goat incident Ron thought it was the best time to bring up once again changing the mascot. It happened at a big meeting with all the campus big wigs present including the new president. Unfortunately for Ron, Beth is once again leading the meeting.

"Alright, I think we can put this incident to rest. No one was seriously hurt and we actually got some good recognition out of it."

Ron smiles, knowing this is going to be his shining moment. He knows that no one understands his self-proclaimed genius and he has to regain some respectability. Say what you will about Ronald Moore but he is passionate. He doesn't want to lose his purchasing abilities. This is the perfect chance to have the mascot changed and gain back some trust.

73

"Well, to add to that…"

Beth doesn't look at him and is already starting to quickly pack up her stuff.

"The meeting has been adjourned."

"I deserve to be heard."

The president doesn't know Ron and his propensity for making bad decisions and decides to step in.

"You're right, go ahead Ron."

"Well, I was thinking that we have to embrace this. It is the perfect time to change our mascot."

Beth sets her jaw and widens her eyes. She doesn't want to look silly in front of the president and wants to show the staff can be professional.

"For the last time Elmer the chicken is not going to happen and I have no idea where we would even get a penguin."

"An evil penguin."

"Yeah, okay…or a Panda Bear."

"A ferocious panda. The team sounds tougher if they have a more badass name. You put evil or ferocious in front of it and the opposing team can't help but be scared."

Beth puts her head in her hands. She just wants to go home to a nice bubble bath and relax. It has been a stressful day and she feels a headache coming on. This is not how she wanted to end her day.

"Our mascot has been around for years. It is a symbol of pride for our school. The students, and more importantly the boosters that give the school money, would be confused and outraged if we just suddenly changed it"

Ron in not deterred.

"I thought about that. Changing our mascot to the goat would bring us great publicity. I have an inside contact with a farm that raises goats and for a small fee they would take care of our chosen one. I would prefer one with a gigantic beard."

Beth looks at the president and gives her a wry smile as if to say I know this all sounds silly but I can take care of this. She turns back to Ron. She wants to subtly let him know that he better stop but Ron doesn't pick up on nonverbal signals very well.

"That is not happening."

Ron is on a roll. I don't think he is even listening.

"We can use it to raise money for the school. We take a couple of goats and put them onto people's lawns. To get them removed they pay us $50. Add that up and we are talking about 1,000s of dollars. It is genius."

"I'm pretty sure that's illegal."

"Actually I checked. The law doesn't mention goats specifically. When I was in jail about ten years ago…"

"Uh, what?"

"Don't worry, I didn't know driving naked was frowned upon and I shouldn't have run from the police. The point is it is not illegal to let an animal wander on to someone else's property and all money goes to a worthy cause."

"Yeah, I don't think so."

"But I already bought the goats."

"What!"

To his dismay, buying the goats becomes Ron's Folly III. His purchasing power is curtailed and henceforward every purchasing decision he makes has to be approved by Beth herself. I look back on college and remember every detail of that day. The next week the school paper had a front-page story of the incident featuring a large picture of a goat chasing down a band member. It was great. A crude video taken from a cell phone appeared on youtube and it was the most downloaded video for several months. It became the topic of conversation and people talked about it for weeks afterwards. It was so cool when friends thought I wasn't there and tried to explain it to me. I would just smile and say I was sorry I missed it.

Soon after the incident, I joined the college debate team, ironically run by Dr. Walker. Things came full circle at a debate tournament later in the semester when I gave a speech about the aggressive and confrontational nature of mountain goats. The average goat has 3 to 4 conflicts with other goats per hour, all year long. They do not butt heads. Rather, they poke each other in the hindquarters or on the backside with their horns. As a result of this constant fighting, male mountain goats have developed an extra-thick layer of skin to protect their behinds. Basically, they are always getting angry and fighting with each other. Dr. Walker sits in the front row, evaluating my performance. As soon as I begin my speech a sparkle of realization sweeps across her face. After collecting her thoughts she smiles slightly. I can't really say why but, for some reason, I wanted her to know. She is the only one that ever figures it out and she never says anything. I had so much confidence after that. I felt like I could accomplish anything and walked around campus like I owned the place. It was a great semester.

DATING

DR. LOVE

To talk about my first dating experiences I take you back to middle school, a time when young boys start to experience dating and all the awkwardness that comes with it. The problem is I was a little dorky and very accident-prone. In sixth grade my class went on a trip to Washington D.C. We went to a high-end clothing store. I am not going to buy anything but I browse through some of the clothing racks when a kick-ass leather jacket catches my eye. You know, I like to keep up with the latest fashions. Plus, the coolest guy in school wears a similar jacket and he has a hypnotic power with the ladies. Perhaps the jacket could give me similar powers. The store is very crowded and it was hard to maneuver through the aisles. I start talking to a girl named Elizabeth in my class by one of the clothing racks. I try on the jacket for her. I'd like to think I am flirting but I'm not really sure how to do it. I am trying to be cool and relaxed but I am super nervous. I am sure I am saying the wrong thing. All of a sudden someone brushes by me and I loose my balance.

I go careening into several clothing racks, knocking them over and knocking over people in the process. I slam my right eye into a metal bar sticking out from one of the clothing racks. As I topple over I see the look of shock on Elizabeth's face. I lie on the floor thinking that once again I screwed it all up and embarrassed myself. When I finally untangle myself and shakily rise to my feet I find the teacher towering over me. She drags me to the front of the store and makes me explain to the clerk what happened. Luckily no damage was caused but for the rest of the trip I have to stand by the teacher's side everywhere we go so I won't cause anymore trouble. My classmates talk about the incident for days afterwards but a black eye does kind of make you look tough. The clumsiness continued with me falling off the stage during a choir performance, getting into a fight with a locker door, and spilling milk all over myself during lunch. Maybe Angus can help me with my clumsiness issues too.

After the clothing rack incident I go to my father for advice. I figure he has a lot more dating experience than I do. He is reading the paper after dinner and contemplating getting a bowl of ice cream for dessert.

"Dad, so there's this girl…"

My dad doesn't look up.

"It's paper time. Go ask you your mother."

"I really like her. I'm not sure how I should act around her."

My dad folds the paper and puts it down next to him on the couch. He smiles broadly.

"Ah, young love. I bet she's a saucy little minks, a challenge for any dewy eyed romantic. If that black eye is from her punching you in the face she likes you. If she beats the crap out of you you might as well make love to her right there on the spot."

I am confused. I stare at my dad trying to figure out what he is saying. He looks away shaking his head.

"Hypothetically, I mean…make love to her hypothetically… wait, I've confused myself…where's your mother?'

"I really like her but I always get nervous and say the wrong thing or fall into something."

"Okay, why do you like her?"

"Oh, she is perfect. She is beautiful in every way. She is so cute when she giggles and…I can't even explain it."

"Son, I am going to tell you something that will help you talk to any girl…everybody poops."

There is a long pause. My dad is getting uncomfortable. I am guessing I look both confused and horrified.

"Look, you have put her on this imaginary pedestal but she is just like everyone else, not some grand being. You may think of her as someone really special but she is no different then you are. She poops just like you."

"Ew…"

"No, listen…"

My dad puts a hand on my shoulder and looks directly into my eyes. I have never seen him look this intense before.

"…Everybody poops."

I have no idea what to say so after a long pause I just walk away. At the time I thought he was just joking around and ignored his comment but now it strongly resonates with me. Every time I become interested and perhaps a little infatuated with a girl I remember what my dad said all those years ago. It is some of the best advice he has ever given me. Back then, I decide he is a kook and need advice from someone my own age. Instead of my father, I decide to use my best friend Angus; we called him beef, to hone my skills. Angus is very suave. He is my dating hero and my suave coach.

He is so confident and he makes talking to girls seem so effortless. Even I am charmed by him. Oddly enough, now in his mid twenties, Angus is broke and living in New York. He also has a drug problem and is dating a hooker named Lolita Mianus. He called me once crying to tell me he has given up on love entirely. His love for women has been replaced with an intense love for crack cocaine. I will always stand by his side in case of trouble though, the terrific duo of suave man and his sidekick the dateless wonder. Damn it, I hate that nickname. I want my buds to call me ballin' Nick K to sound tough but it never quite catches on.

Regardless, I am very excited to get advice from the master. I descend the stairs into what Angus calls the love pad, or what doubles as his parent's basement. I have to admit it is pretty cool. His large bedroom is to the left, with a full bathroom attached. It seems unfair that my bedroom is half the size and I have to share a tiny bathroom with my sister. To the right is a large carpeted room where Angus spends most of his time. On one side of the room there are cushy chairs and a couch surrounding a gigantic plasma T.V. equipped with surround sound. He also owns a ton of DVD's and video games. The rest of the space is filled with some gym equipment, a pool table, large fridge, and a dart board. It is the coolest basement of all time and truly a sign of how much he is spoiled. I have to admit if I were a girl I would be down here as much as possible. There are also strobe lights on the wall that apparently are supposed to set the mood. There are candles everywhere and at least six David Bowie posters on the wall. Angus says when he does impressions of the sexiest rocker alive the ladies dig it. Is this really the kind of environment the ladies like and I wonder if his parents approve? I find out later the supposed love pad has usually been a turn off. Regardless I am ready to learn.

"Alright Nick, Lesson one is very important. Your previous dating experience and advice you have gotten from your family is not important."

It's true that my dating experience has been lackluster. I dated Megan Duffy for three weeks but it ended badly. I was at her house for her birthday party. I made her a homemade card, which I thought was highly creative. It only took me about five minutes to draw balloons and confetti on a folded up piece of paper but I legitimately forgot it was her birthday. I also kept telling Mary that she should have bought a cake I could pop out of singing the "Happy Birthday" song. Popping out of a cake is on my list of things to do before I die. Whether my bride to be wants it or not it is definitely happening at my wedding. She would be like: "where's my husband" and I would pop out of the cake saying: "here I am." It would be so awesome. Then I would sing her "our song". Despite being covered in icing, it would be so romantic. I also had a momentary clumsy moment at her birthday party and accidentally spilled grape juice all over Megan's favorite dress. It didn't go over well, especially considering I couldn't help but laugh. I tried to make up for it by saying I would help her change but she was confused about what I meant by this. Flustered, I insisted that she spill something on me to make up for it. At first she refused but then, of course, dumped a full glass of grape juice over my head. I had no idea what to say next so I had to turn around and walk away. Unfortunately, she was my ride home so I sat covered in grape juice until everyone else had gone home.

"Alright, I can do that."

"Also Nick, I want you to make a commitment to this. If you want this to work it needs to be a priority."

"Done. Can we do some kind of role play or something?"

Angus sighs. This was going to be harder than he thought.

"Fine"

Alright Angus, you are a fourteen year old girl"`

"But I'm not."

"Well, let's just say you are, just for the purpose of this… uh…training session."

"What do I look like?"

Hmmm, I do wonder what Angus would look like as a girl. He is quite muscular for his age and lifts weights to work on his rippling physique. He tried to put me on an exercise program to increase my muscle mass but...uh...it was hard and I am lazy. The rock hard abs I hoped would take me only a couple of workouts never really happened. Angus always has a crisp crew cut that accents his chiseled features. I get my hair cut at SEARS by an old woman named Marge. She looks like she is going to fall over at any minute and I suspect she is blind in one eye. It explains why my hair always seems slightly uneven. She has gotten a bit slow as well. Last time I went to see her she told me I was done before I even sat down. When I told her I had just arrived she asked me why I had taken her cat. I really need to start going someplace else. I admit that Angus is a good-looking guy. Of course he always has to think about looks. The women he dates are all very attractive. Unlike Angus, looks are not the first thing I look for in a girl. I am much more sophisticated and interested in personality and compatibility. Oh, whom am I kidding? I was fourteen. I liked breasts.

"I would say you have long straight blonde hair down to your butt. You are tall, have blue eyes, and like to wear pigtails sometimes but not always. I personally like the velvet scrunchy look. You hold your hands behind your back and look down when you feel uncomfortable. You have the cutest freckles around your nose..."

"Wait, stop. I can't believe this. You are still thinking about her."

"I don't know what you mean. I could be talking about anyone."

"You guys kissed once and it doesn't really count. You flinched and she kissed you on the nose. I bet you haven't even talked to her since."

I am talking about Elizabeth and this is not true, dear reader. When she told me she liked me, she told me I must emphasize, I didn't know what to say. I clammed up and couldn't speak. All I managed were a few mumbles. I really liked her but I couldn't manage to get the words out. When she leaned in for a kiss I did flinch at the last moment and she kissed me on the cheek. It was lovely but the accidental flinch shattered my world. It made me feel uncomfortable and undeserving of such a beauty. After that she thought I didn't like her.

I was jealous of the guy she was interested in after me, Robert. I have had problems with Robert since I met him in first grade. He consistently got gold stars and goodies for doing well in class. He stuck every gold star he received to his desk for all to see. He always mocked me for not getting a star and being as smart as him. He also constantly took my stuff and hid my jacket in the winter. He subtly tormented me all year long. What really irked me was that all the girls liked him and thought he was so cool. In my opinion he is scrawny and has weird looking hands. They are too big for his body and excessively veiny. His legs look like toothpicks and he has a dimple that is way to big for his face. Things became serious one day in late October when I wrote in crayon on his desk "Your hair looks stupid". He flipped his hair at me one to many times. When I went to the bathroom he took my crayon, broke it in half, and put it back on my desk. I took it as a clear sign of aggression. Everything came to a boiling point during parent's day. We made crafts to show our parents. The class was a buzz with Robert's painting of the classroom with renditions of every student. In the rendition of me I had fangs and horns. Everyone thought it was hysterical.

Right then and there he became my arch nemesis. He was the Lex Luther to my Super Man. If things were not bad enough classmates made fun of my craft, an igloo made from Popsicle sticks. When my mom saw what I had made she called me her little Picasso. Great, she compares my beautiful works of art to asymmetrical paintings that make people look like they have fallen into a face distorter. I imagine he never really understood human anatomy. Seeing a mouth above a nose is a sign of unsuccessful plastic surgery if you ask me, just ask Joan Rivers. The teacher, Ms. Karen, referred to Robert's painting as genius and hung it next to the blackboard. It remained there the rest of the year silently mocking me. Ms. Karen called my Popsicle igloo "cute" and I had to take it home.

Seven years and several incidents later I am in his homeroom along with Elizabeth. When Elizabeth and Robert start dating out rivalry is renewed. I came into class one day to find a heart drawn on my desk in purple marker. Inside the heart it says: "Elizabeth + Nick forever". Someone was mocking me and they were not going to get away with it. The handwriting is clearly Roberts. Oh, it is on I thought. In retaliation I take his favorite Pokeman card, the pink dragon that could breathe fire and deal a lot of damage and when he can't find it he cries a little before searching the entire classroom, opening all the cabinets and throwing the contents everywhere. Later in the day I challenge him to a Pokeman game and use the stolen card against him. He gets so upset he leaps at me and we wrestle around on the ground for a second. We are both sent to the principles office. The principal Mr. Turnball is not pleased to see me. It is a little over two years ago that my farther punched Mr. Turnball in his office. Robert is suspended for three days. I smile broadly. Ha ha, point Nick. I have finally won the battle and my arch nemesis has been defeated. To my dismay Elizabeth shows him sympathy and lovingly visits his desk all day long when Robert returns. The next day I faked tears to show her I could be sensitive too but everyone just stares at me and calls me a crybaby. He is so evil.

"Lies, all lies. We have great conversations about…you know, stuff."

"Really, when's the last time you talked to her?"

"Why just this morning she came to my locker…"

"No, she didn't"

Shoot, even when I am being super secretive he knows when I am lying.

"Aha, but it could have."

"No."

Damn it. I am so mysterious yet he can read me like a book. The man has a gift. What irks me though is I really need him right now and he is not being helpful. I decide to change the subject.

"Anyway", I say, "I am going to try and flirt with you. You ready?"

"This is stupid."

"Oh, common. Just bear with me. Here we go. Hey Elizabeth, you are looking pretty today. You are like the sun, I melt when I am close to you"

I put my hand on Angus's shoulder. He pulls back.

"Man, why are you touching me."

"Well, I figure we would have some playful banter and I could put my arm around you or something. Maybe some more banter and I could lean in for a kiss or something."

Angus looks confused.

"Okay, I don't feel comfortable with this."

"What, I need to make this feel real. Now, I put my arm around you and we make eye contact. I say: hey, beautiful. You are my sun…I melt when I am close to you."

Angus pulls back and shakes his head.

"The sun burns. Almost like how you will crash and burn if you use that line."

"It's a great line. I mean what else melts things. Saying she is like a microwave or a hot stove sounds dangerous."

"Man, you are hopeless. You are putting too much thought into this. Look, all you need to do is be yourself. You are a nice guy and witty. Although…"

His voice trails off and he looks down.

"What?"

"Nothing."

"It sounds like you were going to say something. We are friends. I can take it. I promise I won't be offended."

"Fine. I am saying this as a friend. You're a bit of a dork. Don't worry though, we can work on it."

I am shocked. I am the coolest guy I know. I mean I collect action figures but I use them to show my artistic ability. The colors can be dull so I repaint the figures to make them extra vibrant. I am a proud owner of the full star trek collection. I have the limited edition Spock figurine. It is a collector's item and it is glorious. I know guys who get permanent ear extensions and cut their hair to look more like Spock and that is just crazy. I have my standards.

"That is preposterous."

I have to pause for just a second for educational purposes. There are many misconceptions about the differences and similarities between nerds, geeks, and dorks. All three are awkward but in distinct ways and outward appearance has a lot to do with it. A nerd is clarified by their obsession and absolute devotion to certain interests and hobbies. If someone plays games involving mythical creatures he or she is a nerd. If said individual chooses to play as a woodland creature and feels the need to raise their voice an octave in order to do so they are an Uber nerd. If someone wears full armor and fights non-existent elves or dwarfs in public they are beyond hopeless. Nerds can live normal lives while Uber nerds will never have a girlfriend.

A geek can have nerdy interests or hobbies but are smart. They have no athletic ability whatsoever so they get their competition from activities such as chess. They may brag about their chess skills and high IQ's but that is because that is all they have to brag about. Often times they wear glasses and goofy polo shirts. A lot of kids from other countries seem to be geeks. I believe this is a true sign of the state of the education system in our society. Both nerds and geeks can end up stuffed into lockers. A dork is not exceptionally smart and is not characterized by nerdy activities. They never wear matching clothes and will never understand why they don't match. They are very likely to wear socks with sandals and white socks with suits. They are awkward in social situations even though in many cases they don't acknowledge it. They are clumsy and try way too hard with the ladies. Dorks are harder to describe but easy to spot. Put a nerd, a geek, and a dork together and you have one awkward posse.

I once took an online test rating whether I was a nerd, dork, or geek. I scored low on the geek scale, less than 20%. I am clearly not a geek and in fact actually have pretty good athletic ability. I scored much higher on the nerd scale and I do admit my nerdiness does show at times. I do enjoy greeting people with the Vulcan sign. On the dork scale I was off the charts at 95%, with perfect scores in both social awkwardness, and lacking skills with the ladies. It is true that my fashion sense is limited and I hardly ever match. I am a full-fledge dork and am not afraid to admit it. I know it sounds cliqued but it is important to always be true to yourself. We are often afraid of our own thoughts or feelings. Believe me, people can I am glad I could educate you dear reader and I hope this lesson has not been too distracting from the story. Angus needs to think of a way to make his point more understandable.

"Okay, let me ask you this. What are your plans for this evening."

Aha, the perfect opportunity to prove just how cool I really am. I put on my proud face and smile.

"I am going to make myself a cup of hot cocoa with three large marshmallows so they melt into the cocoa. I usually only put in two but three makes it extra creamy and we only live once right. I might watch a movie"

"That's what I thought."

I'm 25 and I still have trouble meeting the ladies. My sister gave me some pretty good advice though. She says collecting action figures is not a turn on. Women my age want a guy that is mature and something that is typically part of childhood is not good. Having a conversation without once mentioning Spock is so hard. He is one of my heroes. I mean Spock represented the best qualities of man, emotionally compassionate and cool and calculating. He saved the universe on many occasions and was a brave and noble representation of the Vulcan race. George Washington crossed the Delaware River and was a decorated general. He was the leader of the country and saved countless lives. Martin Luther King Jr. was the voice of change and inspired thousands of people. They are very important people in American history but even they didn't accomplish as mush as Spock. Captain Pickard with Spock by his side saved the universe on numerous occasions. Who else can say that? Spock inspires me to be great. If admiring a man who helps save the universe and has amazing ears is not cool then I have little hope for our society. His struggle with his human and Vulcan side is universal. I was not adopted but the idea of being from two distinct worlds is a contemporary theme explored more than forty years in a television series that inspired many.

This is without even mentioning the revolutionary scientific ideas the show explored. The concept of the space-time continuum, and beaming between places was revolutionary. If my sister tells me next comic books are not cool I will die a little inside. My sister also told me girls do not like a guy whom is vain and too into his looks. Being the physical specimen that I am it is hard not to admire my perfectly sculpted bod. I kid of course. I have no problem there. My senior year college roommate used to walk around the dorm in his underwear and tell women he was, for a limited time, offering free tickets to his gun show. There were no takers. My sister does seem to give good advice though. I really want Angus to come over. It would be so much fun. It would be male bonding at its finest, a man-date beyond compare.

"You should come over. I believe there is enough Cocoa for two. We can watch a movie while you give me pointers. It will be great."

"I think I will pass."

"You can have four marshmallows."

"No thanks. All right, I can show you my skills but putting them into practice is something else entirely. By the time I am done with you girls will be coming up to you. "

I need a nickname for Angus. I can't call my relationship guru Beef. It sounds weird and oddly inappropriate.

"Sounds good. I will call you Dr. Love. I have a fever and the prescription is some extra attention from the love doctor."

"Okay, that sounds sexual. Lesson number one: Don't be creepy. We have a lot of work ahead of us."

We start on my outward appearance. My makeover starts with my outdated clothes. My look of Kaki shorts and a dress Polo is not as cool as I would hope. I buy faded jeans with rips around the knees. I complete the look with a black leather jacket and dark sunglasses. Black leather shoes complete the look. If I were living in the 60's I would form a band of disgruntled school thugs and challenge the other gang trying to take over the school. Amid awkward dance numbers and off key singing my gang would make idle threats and I would win the heart of the good girl. Or if we lived in a world dominated by machines where robots could be sent back in time I could carry a kick ass shotgun and protect John Conner. In the end I decide the jacket is not the look for me and go with sports jackets instead. Angus also says one of the first things a girl notices about a guy is his shoes. They must be nice but casual.

The next step is proper communication strategy. He first shows me the art of being coy. He explains that I need to act as if I am not interested even if I am. It makes me seem intriguing and different from all the other guys who try and flirt with her.

"Okay, now remember what I taught you. I'll be Elizabeth. So I see you in the hallway and say: hey, how are you?"

"Fine, but I really don't care how you are feeling."

"Uh...let's keep going. What are you up to this weekend?"

I cross my arms and turn my back.

"Anything that doesn't involve you."

"What?"

"Wow, that dress is ugly."

"Stop, stop. You can't be a total jerk. Maybe respond by asking her what she is doing and not act super excited, just interested."

"Yeah, that sounds like a better approach."

"Look, at one time at least she was interested in you. In my opinion she wants to know you still care about her. Be yourself and give her the attention she truly deserves."

It is clear I need more practice. I first try my coyness on Angus's mom. She gives me a weird look and tells me to go home. Despite this setback I decide I am finally ready for the big time. With a new fresh appearance and confidence in my communication technique it is time to test my flirtation skills in the field. My secret weapon is a list of original pick up lines I have written down and secured in my back pocket in case of emergency: "you are like a light bulb…you light up my world", "when I look into your eyes I see the beauty of the universe", and the always reliable "you make me want to believe in love again." I have to brag that I made them up myself. They are all original and Angus guarantees that if all else fails and I am going down in flames they will work.

Angus suggests I start small and try talking to a few girls before asking them out. I decide there is no reason to do so when I feel confidence for the first time. I haven't kept in touch with Elizabeth in the last couple of months because I have felt uncomfortable around her but I am feeling extra confident. At this point in my life she was still the girl of my dreams and it never hurts to try. Not trying and regretting it later is truly a shame. I have learned that lesson too many times over the years. Thank the heavens that Elizabeth finally dumped Robert after months of personal torment. She dated Paul soon after but it did not work out and they recently broke up. Paul was my friend in elementary school and we were close up until several months ago, ironically about the time he started dating Elizabeth. Paul is a nice enough guy, but he is a little nuts. He lives his life based on fortune cookies. He collected as many as he could and stored them in the cabinet next to his bed. Every time he needed guidance he would open a cookie and follow the fortune specifically.

He believed Buddhist monks living in China in the early thirteenth century wrote the fortunes as a message meant for him in this lifetime. He always rambled about building a time machine to visit ancient times and receiving guidance from the source. He even wrote Time Machine on a refrigerator box and sat inside it for hours. Nothing happened and he eventually got hungry and gave up. Paul claimed it was his destiny to live life according to the fortunes. I don't really believe in destiny but I'm pretty sure ancient Buddhist monks wouldn't waste their time on Paul. He got a fortune once that said: "A closed mouth gathers no feet." He didn't talk for a month unless absolutely necessary. When he sat with my friends and I at lunch he would write his thoughts down on a note pad and make me say them to the group. It got so annoying. I got more and more agitated until he wrote that my fangs were showing and threw chopped garlic all over me. Our friendship soured after that. Ironically enough Elizabeth found the incident a turn on and her and Paul started dating soon afterwards. I should have seen this as a sign Elizabeth didn't have feelings for me. Another fortune Paul opened said: "Food sometimes eats itself."

For the record I have no idea what this means and if I saw a cookie eat another cookie I would be sure I was losing my mind. My guess is the fortune is an analogy about survival of the fittest but the analogy is lost on me. Paul thinks this is a comment about cannibalism. He doesn't sleep for months because he is convinced his parents are going to eat him in the middle of the night. He stops eating meat because clearly it must all be human. He comes home one day to find very little food in the house and flips out. He assumes he is on the dinner menu. Needless to say Paul had a few screws loose. His mind seemed to become unhinged all too often. He accused Elizabeth of being from the planet Zenon and trying to steal the world's oxygen to build a new species of super worm. Elizabeth broke up with Paul soon after.

With the relationship with Paul officially on the outs I decide it is the best time to try and show Elizabeth how much I care. Her locker is on the first floor of the school next to the gymnasium. After the bell rings signaling the end of the day Elizabeth walks down the hall and opens her locker. She puts away her books and grabs her backpack to take home. I am about to say hello when another guy jumps in front of me and taps Elizabeth on the shoulder. I stand behind him in shock. I did not expect this. I panic and to avoid the moment I quickly duck as if a bullet is coming at my head. As Elizabeth turns around she looks down and sees me crouching in front of her. The guy just stares at me and shakes his head.

"Nick?"

Well, damn. I was so prepared. My confidence was built up and nothing could stop me. I even had a back up plan. I was going to ask her out and there was no way she could possibly say no. Suddenly everything had unraveled and I was on the floor. I must gather my thoughts. I get up and lean against the lockers. I try and look smooth while re-gathering my confidence but slip and hit my head against the locker. I slide down the face of the locker and crumple onto the floor. Well, that didn't work. I have the urge to walk away like every other time but I get back up and lean against the locker once more. I pick my head up high.

"Oh hey, is your locker in this hallway. That's crazy…I was going to go get my books."

I glance at the guy who stands there confused. He is clearly in awe of my skills. I'll have to give him a couple of pointers later.

"Nick, your locker is on the second floor?"

"Is it? You got me; I'm going to shoot some hoops. I have to practice before the tryouts coming up. Yeah, coach says I'll be a starter."

I am impressed with my save. Maybe I can do this. As if on cue the guy, still standing behind me, feels like he has to chime in.

"Tryouts were weeks ago and you weren't even there. I've seen you play and you suck."

I frown at the guy and he gives me a puzzled look. There is a pause. I stare at the floor as if what I should say next is written there. I clear my throat.

"Well I'm more of a street baller, uh…"

Elizabeth smiles.

"Did you come to flirt with me?"

Oh no, she has found me out. I thought I was being so secretive and allusive. Ah, but what does she mean by this. By saying I am flirting with her does it mean she is in turn flirting with me. I need to say something witty and playful.

"Well, I only flirt with the beautiful ladies."

In my mind I am saying that I am flirting with her and I also think she is beautiful. My interpretation isn't exactly the message she got. I'm pretty sure she thinks I am saying I don't think she is one of the beautiful ones. She frowns. Quick, say something clever. Didn't Angus say I was supposed to notice something? Aha…

"I really like your shoes."

"But…"

I look down and notice she is wearing sandals.

"Damn it. I saw that, I just…hold on one second…"

I reach in to my back pocket and grab the sure fire pick up lines. My hands are shaking. I leaf through them as Elizabeth stands there patiently and the guy stands there confused. I quickly settle on one that I'm convinced will work perfectly.

"You are like the sky on a clear autumn day. You are beautiful and look even better at night."

Elizabeth takes a step back. Hopefully it is in awe of my genius line but she looks confused. Man, I should have gone with the one about the sun and her melting my heart.

"Thanks, but I don't get it. Why at night?"

"Uh..."

I am about to say something when the guy still standing behind me chimes in once again. As a fellow male you would think he would see a man struggling with a lady and either come to his aid or leave well enough alone. I assumed it was part of the bro code but apparently not.

"Dude, that is weak. She is way too good for you man."

"Oh, I am sure you are some kind of Casanova with your abs of steel and chiseled good looks."

"Uh...thanks?"

Another failed attempt. This is the girl I have had a crush on for the longest time. I think I just put way too much pressure on myself. Around her I am too afraid to be me, like I have to be perfect. I could walk away but I don't want to do that this time. I have to remember Angus's lessons and at least not make a total fool of myself.

"Elizabeth, I think you're great. You are beautiful and caring. I just think you deserve the best. Uh...and...I do sorta like you...a lot."

She doesn't say anything for a second. She is smiling and I think she liked what I said. I have to say I am impressed with myself. Sure, it wasn't exactly what Angus had in mind but long speeches work in Shakespeare plays so maybe it can work. Playing it cool is not my strength and I don't want to go against my personal style.

"God that was pathetic. That's your strategy; spouting some sappy BS you probably heard on some Lifetime movie of the month tearjerker. That is a load of crap. You just want to get inside her pants and girls don't like it when you give them some speech about how much you like them."

I shoot the guy a look that could kill.

"Your funeral man"

He walks away and gives Elizabeth a wink. Elizabeth scrunches up her nose.

"Don't worry about him, he's a jerk."

"Yeah, the nerve of that guy."

"You know, I like you too."

I am taken a back.

"Really?"

"Well yeah."

This sounds genuine. I have to be sure though.

"Okay…Did Angus put you up to this? Is there some kind of hidden camera thing, because my feelings are not for sale? Is this some sort of test? Oh, this is over the line. I'll tell you I am going to have to fire him as my love coach. That no good…"

"Nick, I really do."

I contemplate this for a second. She is very believable.

"Are you sure?"

"Well, Yeah."

I smile as I realize this is real. Wow, this is the most amazing feeling in the world. All the anxiety is gone and my heart is light, floating like a wavering balloon in the afternoon breeze. I'm not really sure if Angus's advice really worked but he did give me confidence. Next time I see him I will definitely put four marshmallows in his cocoa.

"Oh, yes…well…do you want to go out for pizza sometime."

"I'd like that."

To this day I have no idea who that guy was or why the hell he winked. I never saw him again after that. I didn't really date Elizabeth for long but we remained good friends all through high school. Even though she is out west living with her boyfriend I still talk to her from time to time. Elizabeth and that memory are still very vivid in my mind and I will always remember it.

GROWING UP

PARENTAL ADVICE GONE WRONG

I wonder what it would be like to have a midlife crisis. The one I am about to tell you about ends with a crazy party that includes my dad claiming he is not the devil and risqué fire dancing. Along the way there is naked pot smoking and a gang of nerds pretending to enact the civil war. The movies make having a midlife crisis so undesirable. It's always the middle-aged man who begins to question what he is doing with his life. The man works at a dead end job; hating the tiny cubicle he inhabits every workday. He grows his hair out long, wears sunglasses because he thinks he looks like a badass, and buys a Porsche to drive around the neighborhood. The man's attitude at work changes. Instead of sucking up to the boss he does things like "accidentally" taking the stapler home with him and stealing sticky notes. He brags about his "sticking it to the man" while losing sleep at night having nightmares about being caught.

There may be jokes about the man having the crisis but there are definitely some positives. It becomes a great excuse for crazy behavior. So I quit my job, ran off to Vegas, blew all my money, and married some girl I met at a casino pool. It's understandable though if I'm having a midlife crisis. It sounds pretty awesome to me. People think excessive drinking and out of control gambling to try and help a man rediscover his love for life is pathetic. I say "how dare you" to all the naysayers. Everyone needs to let loose once in a while. Sitting in a tiny cubicle and thinking about doing something extreme is healthy. I am not advocating all the men middle-aged men across the country quitting their jobs to go live on the outback with the natives and Kangaroos, but I am saying they should not rule it out. Cliff diving and scuba diving with sharks would be more realistic.

My planned mid life crisis would be awesome. When I get bored with my life and need a change I will start by purchasing my own private island to get away from it all. I have done research and the best available islands for purchase are in the Philippines. My island would feature white sandy beaches and a tropical atmosphere. There would be an abundance of wildlife all over the island including exotic varieties of birds and fish. There would be great locations for snorkeling and scuba diving. I would build the perfect vacation home on one side of the island with easy beach access. The house would feature all the amenities including a screened in porch with beautiful views on all sides and a state of the art kitchen. A hired chef would make delicious meals using fresh plants and exotic fruits native to the island. The best part of the house would be a downstairs study in the back of the house.

You never hear anything about a woman having a mid-life crisis. At age forty I guess they can be considered over the hill but that is not even true these days. I don't understand why these men are judged so harshly. Dad's midlife crisis was quite profound. Among other things he joined a nudist group, which in a smaller town means half a dozen men sitting naked in a room discussing philosophy. They eat doughnuts and relate their lives to the teachings of Niche. When my dad told me about what the group talked about it peaked my interest. I assumed it was just a philosophy club and it sounded interesting. I got extremely restless one evening and decided to check it out. It is not at all what I expected. I walk in the room and stop dead in my tracks. My mind swirls and I am overcome with horror and pain. It is an image I will never get out of my mind.

About ten Middle-aged men are sitting in a circle on folding chairs and totally nude. They are all gradually losing their graying hair if not bald and several are well into their sixties. At a certain age the body no longer holds its natural form and it is clear these men gave up the hope of being aesthetically pleasing long ago. One man is very overweight with pinkish skin. He is completely bald. He looks like a discolored bowling ball. Another man is overly thin and wears oversized square glasses. He sports an uncared for mustache and quite frankly looks like a decrepit porn star way past his prime. I try so hard not to look down. My brain fights my head for control but my morbid curiosity takes control and I catch a quick peek before jerking my head back up. Damn it brain, you have won this time. I turn around to run but my dad's voice stops me.

"Hey, son. What are you doing here?"

My dad gets up and starts walking towards me.

"Oh god. Please don't get up. What the hell is going on here?"

The ugly naked men are staring at me and I am feeling uncomfortable. I have no choice but to look at their frowns and I get a knot in my stomach. I have seen my dad in awkward situations before. He got drunk one night at a party at our house and danced to the song "Roxanne" with his fiend Berry. They were clutching each other and crying. He tried to explain by saying he was trying to recapture his youth but I have never understood the incident. The other guests got unnerved and the party ended quickly. At least he wasn't naked that night. The bigger pinkish skinned man chimes in.

"We're naked"

Wow, way to state the obvious. It turns out he has a PhD in microbiology but chooses to work at a local clothing free sauna. He says it is what he was meant to do and he constantly compares himself to a Greek God. Ironically, a young kid working for minimum wage at the sauna strives to get a PhD in microbiology and make a difference. He wishes he wasn't in a dead end job that keeps him from accomplishing his dreams.

"I gathered that."

The pinkish man strokes his chin and looks deep in thought. Damn, here comes the philosophy.

"Although, perhaps you see us as naked but we really aren't. In an attempt to make sense of a group of middle-aged men that sit around and discuss the important issues of our time you imagine us naked. It's prejudice of you to make such an assumption. It's just like Einstein's theory of relativity. It's all how you look at it."

Wow. Is that supposed to be good philosophy? Is that the kind of false thinking this group was promoting?

"But you are naked. I'm not just loopy over here, it's straight up fact."

"According to you. Remember Einstein's teachings."

What? I just don't understand why they are naked. I mean, I think talking about deeper issues is great but middle-aged men aren't meant to be naked. Wasn't it Freud who said outer nakedness reveals an individual's inner nakedness, or something like that? I think he meant some people are meant to be naked and others are not. Plus, why is it typically ugly men that belong to nudist colonies? I've never heard about attractive females strutting their stuff at beaches across the country. It's almost as if guy's show up to a nude beach expecting attractive females only to find middle-aged men that look exactly like them. At first they are disappointed, but after a refreshing swim and some time to let it all hang out they say to themselves "Ah, what the hell" and decide to hang out for awhile. The freedom of it all is very exciting.

Another possible explanation for the all male nudist groups is the difference in how men and women choose to relax. A woman will come home from a long day at work, sip some red wine, and perhaps take a bubble bath. A man will immediately turn on the ballgame, make himself a sandwich, and take off his pants. I have to admit, it's a great way to spend a lazy Sunday afternoon. Even as I type this I have the urge to take off my pants, but I figure the other people in the coffee shop won't like it. Plus, a guy may think if he takes his pants off she will too. If a girlfriend of mine ever complains I just say, "Well, maybe you should join me." When I dream about nude beaches I think of white sandy beaches with sultry Brazilian women wearing nothing but a smile. That is what it is all about. I am all for being comfortable with your body but only if it doesn't scare kids. If everyone you pass is screaming in horror there is a problem.

There are only two reasons for men to wear string bikinis. One: it is part of some Halloween costume. Even in this case there are several ground rules. Looking at said man in bikini cannot cause sickness or have the chance of causing sickness. This is a judgment call and I ask only that people use their best discretion. Another general rule is the string bikini must be part of a costume and played for humor. If a guy violates either of these rules they can be asked to leave. If a guy walks around in public in a bikini flexing his muscles and feeling sexy he must be stopped. It makes other guys look bad and it's just plain wrong. Two: a man can wear a string bikini if they are insane and think they are either fully clothed or some kind of animal has ripped their clothes off. In this case I feel justified in giving them a pass. Attractive women can wear whatever they want, or don't want, which is extremely encouraged. Old fat men belong in front of the television eating stale chips and sipping a cold beer. They belong indoors fully clothed so there is no chance of seeing too much skin. Hot Brazilian babes are meant to be naked. When out in public it is their duty to drop their top. My dad motions towards an empty fold out chair.

"Gary couldn't make it. Why don't you join us?"

Despite his smile, this sounds ominous. I imagine this is how everyone gets sucked into a cult. This was officially getting creepy. When he speaks again I imagine him with a deep dark voice like Darth Vader.

"Nick, I am your father. Give in to the power of the dark side. We can get naked, smoke some grass, and discuss how we can get rid of the emperor. If not I can just force choke you, but it's really up to you."

It almost sounds like the group decided to kill Gary and it is my destiny to take his place. I don't want that kind of pressure. I wonder if I am going to get some sort of welcoming gift. Maybe I could get a free T-shirt or a bumper sticker. It could say: "Where nakedness is a way of life." My first thought was: "Where nakedness is only the beginning" but that leaves a lot open for interpretation and I don't want to know where it ends. Since I am still looking for a job, I wonder if I could be the group's marketing expert. I have some great ideas for free giveaways and special promotional events. My dad was basically inviting me to get naked with him and discuss matters of philosophical importance. If this is his idea of father son bonding then I don't want anything to do with it. Its like if your dad takes you to a strip club and you both end up getting lap dances sitting next to each other.

I mean, what do you even talk about. You could talk about how nice the weather has been lately without making eye contact I guess. A storm front is moving in and man this feels great. An even bigger decision is how much you let on that you really like it. Because it's your dad and you might feel awkward, you could make a joke about it by perhaps joking that the lap dance girls might still be in high school. When his laugh turns into a look of deep concern it is time to change the subject. You could maybe high five your dad and make funny faces while it's happening to show it was such a good idea to do this. When your dad becomes your wingman in picking up the ladies you have officially become creepy and sad. Regardless, I cannot imagine anything more awkwardly horrifying. Well, perhaps I can. If there was anything I could imagine beyond the realm of thought or occurrence it was this. Trying to forget this moment will most likely take years of intense therapy. I am a consumet bro and I try my hardest not to cry in the face of horror but I can't help but shed a tear.

"I want to go home", I whisper to myself, "I just want to go home."

I turn to leave but my dad grabs my shoulder.

"You can't tell your mother about this."

"You mean she doesn't know?"

I warn you dear reader that I shudder remembering the following conversation. I have never really had the sex talk with my parents. There was the time my dad told me I was dropped off on the doorstep by a stork but that doesn't count. Then there was the time my dad felt embarrassed so he only used hand gestures, which I didn't understand at the time.

"Your mother and I hardly ever have sex anymore…"

"I don't want to talk about this."

I am already trying to cover my eyes so I don't have to see any inappropriate nakedness and now I want to cover my ears too. The other naked men stare at the two of us.

"The only times we do it's nothing but FoSex."

The only time if have heard the term Fo used is in terms of food. A great example is Fo crab, a fake imitation crabmeat that in reality tastes nothing like the real thing. I am racking my brain to try and figure out what the hell my dad is talking about. He has a puppy dog face as if he has just peed on the sofa again.

"Dad, I have no idea what that means, but…"

"It means the sex is so bad your mother can't help but fake it."

Oh dear god. I look at the guys in the circle. They all have goofy smiles on their face and are nodding in agreement. Is this really what men do when they get older I wonder. If so I don't want anything to do with it.

"Okay, I can't do this."

I start to walk towards the door. My dad calls after me.

"Between that and work there is so much stress, you know. I need to just relax sometime"

All the middle aged naked men are nodding in agreement. It suddenly hits me that in a way this is some sort of weird cult. It is a group of people who gather in a ceremonial place. Have I just escaped a fate more horrible than death, a pledge to lead a life filled with unnecessary nakedness and the remembrance of broken dreams? If I find out later a new member was sacrificed I will officially be freaked out. I wonder if there is some kind of bizarre initiation process or hazing ritual that takes place before someone can become a member. I remember my days in college and some of the things fraternities and sororities did to new members. There is always the classic making them drink too much. Some fraternities made them streak around the campus in the dead of winter. Aha, once again the nakedness. I sense a theme.

I never tell my mom about the nakedness and I wonder if she suspects anything. She tells me on more than one occasion that I should go again and it would be fun. I tell my mom I have plans to gouge my eyes out instead. She never questions it, just giving me a weird smile like she knows and thinks it's hilarious but doesn't want to spoil my dad's fun. Three weeks after the naked philosophy incident my dad travels to Arizona for what he says is a business conference. I know immediately they are going for alternative reasons when naked fat man is invited to go along. Two weeks later they come back and my dad is noticeably tanner, has a beard, and has bought a CD featuring Indian flute music. That night I sit on the couch watching MASH, my dad's favorite show. I enjoy the show but not the hour-long lecture about the mistakes the country made during the Vietnam War. Apparently the show can be quite intoxicating. A friend, Mike, once told me his dad didn't go to the hospital to see him born because he was watching the final episode. I imagine this will happen many times in his life.

"I know it's your wedding day Mike. I can't go. You don't understand, I'm watching MASH."

"See your baby. Damn it, MASH is on. How could you be so selfish?"

"I am not seeing you in the hospital. MASH is more important."

This may seem crazy but really explains a lot. The show also reminds me both my parents were avid protestors. My mom participated in sit-ins and sang songs of peace with a flowered wreath on her head. My father smoked marijuana and complained about the "man". They met at a Rolling Stones concert. My dad turns to me during a commercial break and furrows his brow.

"I want to talk to you about something really important son."

Whenever he says this the conversation inevitably gets weird. A large knot is starting to gather in my throat. I have no desire to talk about sex, nakedness, or any combination of the two. If he mentions one more thing about my parent's sex life I think my head will explode.

"I don't think I want to know..."

"I never went to a conference. My buds and I took a road trip out west in Uncle Berry's van..."

Uncle Berry is crazy. When I was 15 we all got kicked out of a football game because he was drunk and throwing peanuts at the female security guard. When we went out west he complained the mules we road down into the canyon on were being mistreated and tried to ride away on one. He didn't get far before park security picked him up. On a beach trip he broke the table leg off the coffee table in the dining room and smashed a guys windshield in for being a better dancer. He may be insane but damn it, that man is fun to hang out with. I never know what he will do next. Uncle Berry is also a hippy. Him and my dad used to party hard in their younger days. The van is covered with pretty colors and peace symbols.

"That sounds fun."

"It was great. I haven't done anything like that since college. It was like time hadn't passed and we were reliving our old adventures."

My dad stares off for a second, no doubt having flashbacks of how things used to be.

"Times were different. I remember I used to smoke with my professor after class. Oh, she was something else. You ever bag a professor?"

I shift uncomfortably in my seat. Instead of the sex talk I always got stories like these.

"Her desk was too small…"

My dad pauses and looks at his hands, turning them over as he speaks. He is deep in thought.

"…and she had these really tiny hands…"

My dad suddenly stops and looks at me.

"Welp, not important. I'll tell you one thing though. You can have your Jonas Brothers. I watched Pink Floyd play an outdoor concert in the pouring rain chugging beer and stage diving into the crowd.

That does sound awesome.

"I felt so alive in those days. Things have become so routine. I needed a change. You know what I mean."

I believe it is true that people have their own way of rediscovering their passion and zeal for life.

"Yes I do."

"When we finally got to Arizona we wanted to find a place where we could kick our feet up and relax. We found this awesome Indian reservation where we lived in tepees. We listened to great music that wafted through the camp every night. One morning I took a walk and saw wild horses running in the distance."

Hmmm, thank goodness. This sounds much better than I imagined.

"You know dad, that actually sounds pretty cool."

"Well, that didn't last long. There was an incident."

My dad lives for incidents. I sometimes think he seeks them out to make his life more interesting. Just last month my dad got into a huge argument with the next-door neighbor over a sycamore tree. They both claimed the tree was on their property. My dad took a chain saw and cut off a limb just to show how serious he was. The logic was that if the neighbor won the war over whose tree it was the missing limb would anger him.

"I was smoking and…"

"You don't smoke."

"Yet."

"So…"

"Son, I need you to pay attention. I had a little too much Indian wine and stumbled into one of the tepees. Needless to say it caught on fire. There was screaming and lots of cursing which I'm pretty sure is not the Indian way. Todd got a little crispy, made worse because he was naked."

I have so many questions. Apparently my dad has taken up smoking now. He once claimed proudly he was going to start smoking a pipe and build himself a study in the basement. The fact that he doesn't have enough books to fill a single bookshelf let alone an entire study was deemed irrelevant. He went around the entire week speaking with a British accent and saying things were pure "poppycock". In the end the study was never built and the pipe he did buy sits in a desk drawer in his office. It only comes out when he wants to impress new workers by saying he is an English Gentlemen He then invites them to Shamdangle with him down to the local pub for a pint of ale. I have tried to explain on many occasions that "Shamdangle" is not a word in any country or any language but then he calls me a Wanker and says I am ignorant of the culture. I also wonder how in the world a cigarette could catch a tepee on fire.

"Dad, none of this makes any sense."

"It was quite the debacle. Relaxing Indian flute music was playing throughout the camp as people were running around in panic. I watched as a high standing tepee fell over and Todd ran by on fire. An Indian Chief riding a white majestic horse rode by and poured a bucket of water on Todd to put out the flames. It was a scene right out of a cowboys and Indians movie."

I'm still confused. I also have no idea what Indian wine is. Do they make their own wine as part of a tradition or something? I imagine Native Americans sitting in tepees drinking perfectly aged Shiraz from wine glasses. They eat aged cheese delicately combined with smoked salmon and placed on crackers. They discuss their love of yachting and delicately comb their $1.000 haircuts. In reality I'm sure the naked philosophy crew brought the wine in themselves and this was the source of the problem. My dad has still not mentioned how one man smoking could burn down a whole camp.

"But, how did everything catch on fire."

"Indian hair is extremely flammable."

"What? Yeah, that sounds racist."

My dad stops and gives me a sideways glance. He adjusts himself and continues unfazed.

"You're missing the point. We had to leave and went down the road to a hotel. It was kind of a dump actually. We gathered…"

"And you got naked…I accept the fact that you get nude with your weird friends. I really don't need to hear this."

"Sam, you do need to hear this. This is a very important lesson."

I can't possibly imagine what kind of life lesson I am supposed to learn from this. There is no way I am going to reach a tough place in my life and think: "my dad set a Native American camp on fire and got naked with his friends; now I know what I want to do with my life." It doesn't seem plausible. Against my better judgment I am going to give my dad the benefit of the doubt.

"Alright, I'm sorry. Continue."

"It just so happens that everyone was naked, but it was secondary nakedness. We decided to smoke some pot. It reminded me of college, having to put a towel under the door to keep smoke from getting out. As I took a drag from the joint and looked through the lingering smoke to see naked men munching on Cheetos, the crumbs falling into ungodly parts of their body, I realized; holy crap, I am having a midlife crisis."

I sit there for a second and don't say anything. Wow. I am truly stunned. I want to laugh at the absurdity of it all but I know this is supposed to be serious. The imagery swirling around in my mind is intense. Old men laughing and joking with smoke swirling around them. In my head they all look so happy. The world has melted away and they are lost in the moment for the first time in years. Their troubles have been buried and for the briefest of times the mind is clear. It's beautiful really.

"The point is, never lose sight of the ones you love. I thought I needed to drastically change my life to be happy. I realize now I just need to appreciate how good I really have it. I don't love those naked men nearly as much as your mother, you, and your sister."

Well, I should hope not.

"Son, I don't need to get naked and smoke pot to appreciate all the beauty in my life. Don't hold back. Go on your own adventures and discover what happiness means for you.

I never thought my dad would ever say anything poignant. Here it was though, I am face to face with an idea I cannot ignore. I finally get it. A midlife crisis is not sad or a sign of weakness. It is an opportunity to rediscover yourself. People make lists of what they want to do before they die and somehow use it as a checklist. Not only was the bucket list a stupid movie but also the message is lost on me. Shouldn't every day be lived to the fullest instead of waiting until the last moments of life to really let loose. If I get to the end of my days and have a long list with nothing crossed off will I feel like I have somehow failed myself. I don't want to sit around and regret I never went skydiving or saw the Pyramids. Life is an adventure and I am going to embrace it. Sure I don't need a group of naked men to show me the path but if that works for my dad I accept it. I smile.

"Thanks dad."

"Oh, uh…and don't smoke pot. It always gets me into trouble. Somehow when I do it I always end up naked."

"That is good advice. Believe me, I…"

"Although it was quite the scene. Maybe not like when I punched your principal in the face, but man…Do you remember that?"

"Oh, I do."

There is a pause.

"And I'm sorry I told you about your mom and I, you know."

"Already forgotten."

There is another pause. He gets up and walks into the kitchen. I relax and breathe out slowly until he pops his head back in one final time.

"And it was inappropriate to talk about that professor…"

"Seriously, I get it. Please leave now."

My dad is a little crazy and needed to burn down an Indian camp to truly see himself but he wasn't afraid to take the journey. Life can devolve into drudgery and predictability. I need to go on great adventures, challenge myself to try new things. I need to find something that gives me that thrill that makes me feel so alive. I'm in a rut and finding that one thing could change everything. My dad also didn't listen to the naysayers and conform to society's norms. He recognized sometimes you have to lose yourself to truly be found. I think being myself is somehow not good enough. Instead of worrying about defining who I am I need to look around and realize I have set up a pretty good life for myself. Sure I haven't established my life quite yet. I am still developing and learning. I am going to school to develop my skills and get a job in something I love to do. It is something to be proud of. Along the way I want to have a few adventures and live the life I want to live.

THE FEARSOME FIVE

When he turned 61 my dad's friend Berry quit his modestly successful career as an investment banker, bought an old church van, and toured around the country following the band U2. His kids had officially left the nest a long time ago and he was fresh off a divorce from his now ex-wife Merlyn. He figured it was the perfect time to go on an adventure of epic proportions to rekindle his desire to live life on the edge and recapture his youth. Some people travel the world and experience other cultures but instead Berry wanted to rediscover America by once again becoming a hippie.

He painted multicolored stripes and tons of peace signs all over the van. He bought a lot of candles and tons of incense to make his van smell like sandalwood. It worked until knocked over candles burnt up the shag carpeting. Berry attempted to grow out his hair, but his receding hairline proved to be a problem. He was so upset from his failed attempts to grow hair, he bought a flowing wig. I actually know a guy who makes wigs and going to his house scares the crap out of me. One tiny room in his house is filled with manikin heads of all different sizes, shapes, and colors. Thinking it was the bathroom, I went in there once late at night and screamed when I was confronted with over 100 human heads staring back at me. I couldn't find the light switch right away and for a second I thought they were real. Luckily, Berry is not a wig maker as evidenced by the poorly crafted one he still sometimes wears.

Berry refused to believe the 70's were over and it was weird and oddly creepy for a man his age to try and relive his youth. He misses the days of wearing baggy clothes and standing outside in the pouring rain to rock out to his favorite band. He never understood sitting in a large arena and waiving glow sticks in support of a group of guys that look like they just came out of the womb. Berry did go to a Jonas Brothers concert to see what the younger generation was listening too. Sitting among an audience of screaming young girls he felt really creepy and security was keeping a close eye on him. When he pulled a lighter from his pocket and waved it back and forth pretending he was rocking out to a heavy rock band, security tackled him and dragged him away. The major problem for Berry is things just aren't like they used to be. On several occasions he drove around the neighborhood and when he spotted people who seemed to share his new found love for life, he rolled down the window and asked if they wanted to party. Neighbors got concerned and Berry was questioned by police.

He didn't understand why people got so creeped out. Berry was happy touring the country until he realized U2 band members weren't the hardcore rockers he hoped they would be and he didn't fit in with the other groupies. The good old days of carefree partying and free love were over and berry went home dejected. Without any income to speak of and no discernable skills he was actually living out of his van for a period of time. It was a rough time for Berry. I advised him to look to the internet to make some money. I read in the news recently an English gentleman that was homeless for more than 15 years put his life up for auction on E-Bay. He sold his years of living on the streets, his ability to juggle whatever he could find for money, his underground training as a street performer, a tattered box he had been living in for several days, a worn mattress, a rusted spoon whittled down into a stabbing weapon, a wilted bouquet of roses he had found in a dumpster, his beard, a tattered trench coat he wore when he walked around pretending to be an English dignitary, a self portrait drawn in purple crayon, a letter officially stating he had the right to sleep with the queen signed by her in the same purple crayon, a charred match he had used to burn down the box house of a rival and quite cantankerous homeless man, an eye patch, and many years worth of police beatings.

Apparently he had created an account using a computer in the public library and decided he needed to do something drastic to change his situation. He only expected to make a few dollars. A month later he was shocked to discover his life had been bought for $33,000. Soon after he collected his money he was able to rent an apartment with the money and has gotten a job as a Wal-Mart greeter. Unfortunately, the guy that made the purchase thought it was a joke and didn't think he would actually have to pay. After a drawn out civil lawsuit he lost all his savings he spent years building up, was forced to sell his house, and now lives in a modest apartment.

Reportedly, he was recently fired from his job and now works as a Wal-Mart greeter at the very same Wal-Mart. Surprisingly, there is no bad blood between them. They share the same shift and swap stories about their former lives. I told Berry he should put his life up for sale on E-Bay too but he just starred at me. Who knows, people may bid on his life story and worldly possessions. Who would not want: Berry's used wig, his battered van, his shattered hopes and dreams, a snow shovel, an old candy bar wrapper, a broken metal detector, a broken heart, a large golden Gong, a crossbow (don't ask), a UFO detector (really don't ask), a fart machine (really really don't ask), and a box of matches. Yeah, Berry is delicately walking the line between sanity and insanity and I doubt he would get many bids.

I also told Berry he could write a book about his experience. I know a guy who was homeless since he was a teenager, until he decided to document his experiences on computer paper he took from the town library. His memoir, "Living Homeless" was a huge hit and even made it briefly on the bestseller list. According to the books inside jacket cover, it is the emotional tale of a man who, against all odds, put his self-destructive ways behind him and rose out of the gutter to lead a blessed life. It is a story of heartache, desperation, determination, and ultimate triumphant in a tale that will challenge our beliefs about those less fortunate than ourselves. It's quite gripping and, especially in this economy, I recommend it. Recently, he has been a frequent guest on Oprah and has inspired millions of people around the country. Last I heard, "Living Homeless" is being made into a movie starring Robert Downey Jr. If nothing else Berry could write about his attempts to become a hippy again and the life lessons he learned along the way.

In the end, Berry did not live out of his van for long. Luckily, he did end up finding temporary work and his parents felt guilty so they let him live in the house in town for the summer while they stayed in a rented beach house. To get himself back on track Berry knew he had to find a way to bring back the happiness of his younger days. Without a job and desperate for cash Berry rented out his basement to several what he thought were college students. I began to hear stories and rumors about them from my dad and others in the neighborhood. Stories about their exploits began to grow. The first thing I heard was allegedly they were members of a local gang that was consistently causing mischief around the area.

I've also heard they ride around on supped up motorcycles and challenge other motorcycle gangs to street races. They win every time. They have won every race and have quickly established dominance in the area. When the rival gang tries to beat them up to send a message they get whooped. In essence, they are really tough guys and everyone in the neighborhood is afraid of them. If the mafia were still prevalent they would be the top family sending out hits on rival families. They hold gang rallies in Berry's basement and I've heard if anyone attends without an official invite they are banned from certain locations around town including the ice skating rink and arcade. They value their unanimity, so they are rarely seen. Rumors of their accomplishments travel like whispers on the wind.

I did have a run in with the gang only once and it was a memorable experience. It is the winter of my freshman year in college and I am home for Christmas break. My dad, Berry, his son, and I are going to a football game to watch my favorite team play a game with playoff implications. I am very excited and hopefully Berry can show he is finally over his van phase. When my dad and I arrive at Berry's home we honk the horn but no one is coming out. I wonder where they are. I knock on the door and ring the doorbell but it doesn't seem like anyone is home. They could already be at the stadium but we have the tickets. I hear dramatic instrumental music coming from inside the house. I know this is not what either Berry or the son listen too. I would expect either classic rock or classic 80's tunes. I imagine the fearsome five would be listening to hard core metal or grunge. I open the front door and follow the music to the basement. The fearsome gang must be in the basement drumming up mischief.

I am scared to open the door for fear of what I might see but they probably know where Berry is. As I open the door, smoke swirls up the steps and I get a big wif of lilacs mixed with dust. Not exactly the smell I would have thought but even gang bangers like things to smell nice. I still expect to find young men dressed in chains and leather drinking whiskey straight from the bottle and talking about the next crimes they are going to commit. As I descend the stairs I see a fake castle in one corner of the room complete with a rope drawbridge. Around the castle are fake rocks, trees, and fences. It looks like a medieval battlefield. This is in direct contrast to the posters of scantily clad women cluttering the walls. What the hell is going on here?

As I get to the bottom of the stairs I see three pimply-faced teenagers sitting on a red couch cheering. In the center of the room stand two other teenagers facing off in fierce battle. They are circling each other, fake swords at the ready. They are all dressed in full armor. A rack of fake swords rests in the corner. The only thing missing is a real horse tied to the railing. I can't believe it. These are the dangerous biker guys that supposedly cause mischief all across town? The gang feared by police and every rival group with even a thought of causing trouble for fear of retaliation? I could probably take them on all by myself with no arms and a helmet covering my eyes. Then again looks can be deceiving. The awkward teens hear my footsteps on the stairs and immediately freeze.

"Hey guys. My dad and I are supposed to be going to the game with Berry. Have you seen him?"

The guys just look at each other. No one says anything for what seems like forever. All you can hear is the squeak of the armor when they move. One of them inches closer to the swords and I catch the glint off of one of the blades. My heart is pounding and suddenly I think that these guys really might be for real. Speaking through his metal helmet one of the crew sounds a little like Darth Vader.

"You should not be here. It would be wise for you to turn around and forget everything you have seen here."

I feel like I'm in an episode of the twilight zone. Every one of them looks so serious. I eye the rack of swords nervously. Maybe they are real after all. What are the odds that they are all black belts in karate or something and are experienced swordsman? If they turn out to be ninja assassins; however, I can acknowledge their skills and accept my fate. I quickly come to my senses and assess what I am dealing with. They all probably think they are some sort of mythical creature and are not a threat. Maybe if I tell them I am a wizard with magic powers any fisticuffs can be avoided. Then again, maybe this is what the Fearsome Five do in their spare time. They do this to unwind from a long day of mischief and agitation. It is a cover for the blackness within.

Or, could this be an elaborate trap. The Fearsome Five are using these guys as bait. Not wanting people to know their true identity they hid as soon as they heard someone open the basement door. They could be hiding around the room right now, ready to pounce if I come down the stairs any further. One more step and I could be a casualty of their secrecy and unanimity. I am now afraid and my hands are shaking. I turn around to leave but pause. My curiosity is killing me and is overwhelming my fear of impending danger. I have to know what is happening here even if it means my certain peril. I descend the stairs as the teenagers stare at me without saying anything.

"Um, okay. I don't know what is going on here, but…"

One of the teenagers takes of his helmet and places it under his arm. He has short red hair and lots of freckles. He wears thin-framed glasses.

"Do you know who we are?"

What a weird question. I assume they are referring to the group's reputation. I am afraid if I say yes they will have to make sure I am not a member of a rival gang. I am too young to be tortured for information. Who knows what kind of torture it could be? The group could also be concerned I will snitch on them and reveal their true identities and where they hang out to everyone. If they know it was me that gave away their secrets what will they do with me? If I say no maybe I can get out of here in one piece but it could be a trap. I decide silence is the way to go until one of them moves closer to the rack of swords.

"Well…I have heard stories. I'm sure you guys are gentle natured. I never believe what I hear, you know."

"We are going to have a chat. Excuse us."

The five teenagers gather and whisper to each other. Every now and then they turn and look at me. The discussion gets heated as they decide what to do with me. I hear several of them whispering that they shouldn't let me leave and I will tell everyone. I have no idea what they are talking about. I stand there not knowing what to do. The leader of the pack, whom I later learn is named Thomas Peoples, walks slowly towards me.

"Can I get you a beverage?"

"How about a stiff drink?"

I laugh but realize I am the only one.

"We don't drink, I mean we are all underage."

I am totally confused. I thought these guys were antiauthority. They would be drinking and causing a ruckus just because they could. They would be smoking cigarettes and flicking the butts at pools of gasoline just for kicks. They wouldn't care about rules or what society dictated. Something is totally wrong here. They must be making me feel comfortable so they can really show how fearsome they can be.

"Look, I really don't want to cause any trouble. I'm not from a rival gang and I will never bother you again."

"What have you heard about us exactly?"

Man, I need to get out of here.

"Well, I am going to be on my way. If you see Berry tell him I am going to be at the football game. Anyways you guys have a nice day...doing...whatever it is you do. So..."

I turn around but Thomas is blocking the stairs.

"What's your name?"

I can't speak for a second. My voice comes out high and squeaky.

"Nick"

"Come, sit with us for a second."

"I don't think so..."

Thomas looks menacing.

"I insist."

"...okay then."

I sit on an old dusty red couch that should be at a garage sale somewhere. They slowly take off the armor they were wearing and set it on a rack in the corner of the basement. I am shocked to see five pimply-faced high school kids. I assumed they were tough looking beefy men sporting tattoos and short haircuts. Instead they look like a wimpier, if that's possible, Jonas Brothers Band. I'm not sure whether to be sad or really angry. I thought it would be thrilling to encounter a gang of such fierce stature. I am left empty and disappointed. Even I was a little nervous of these guys and avoided certain places in town because they were known as the gang's hangout. If these really are the guys what the hell have I been missing out on? Two of them sit on either side of me. Thomas sits on a folding chair in front of me.

"The thing is, we are known as the notorious fearsome five, a rough and tumble thug group that controls the neighborhood."

The house is nestled in the woods with nature on all sides. There is wildlife everywhere, including a lake that brings out the vacationers. The other two houses in the area are owned by elderly couples. Mr. Potter next-door gets cranky sometimes. He decided a long time ago he didn't want to know what was happening outside his own little world. He called the paper to tell them he no longer wanted the paperboy to deliver to him. He was alarmed to find his request was refused and the paperboy still came the next day. Despite a slew of angry letters to the newspaper and countless complaints the paperboy kept coming and each morning Mr. Potter would watch from his porch and scowl. The only thing that is missing is a young boy wearing a goofy stripped T-shirt shooting at Mr. Potter with his slingshot. Eventually Mr. Potter got so fed up he thought he needed to take a stand. The next time the paperboy came Mr. Potter burst out from his hiding place behind the mailbox and threw yesterday's paper at the boy. The boy fell off his bike and Mr. Potter screamed at him.

"How do you like it you stupid paperboy. You tell the newspaper that if they send anyone out here again they will be extremely sorry."

The boy never entered the neighborhood again. I have heard that Mr. Potter is on the payroll and makes sure no one comes close to the group's hideout. The other neighbor is an elderly lady who allegedly handles the group's finances. She lives with her younger grandson. No one is sure what he officially does but he is called 'The Enforcer' and allegedly carries a double barreled shot gun so he can really get his point across. They do seem to control the town though. They eat for free at many of the restaurants in town and they even get a discount at local shops. There are so many rumors but I have never seen or heard of any conclusive evidence. I don't believe anyone has seen any of them around town either. They either send out other people to do their bidding or get by simply on word of mouth.

"I've heard about you guys but I don't understand. You guys are supposed to be tough not scrawny teenagers."

The gang laughs. Thomas scoots his chair closer.

"You know looks can be deceiving."

"Okay, I guess, but…"

"Let me ask you this…"

Thomas motions to me.

"Nick."

"Ah, yes. Let me ask you this Nick…why are we supposed to be tough "

"Well, I mean you eat for free at a lot of the restaurants in town because they don't want to get on your bad side…"

The Fearsome Five laugh. I turn around and look at their smiling faces but continue unfazed.

"You collect money from various establishments every month, almost like a ransom, and tell them they have bought your protection. I don't know why they need protection, but…"

The Fearsome Five laugh again. Thomas strokes his chin.

"Listen, Nick…"

Suddenly I hear a baby crying. I look around confused. Thomas stops grinning and cocks his head to one side as if he is also confused. Thomas blinks away the crying and tries to continue as if he can't hear it.

"Uh, you see…it's all just based on rumors. People trust what they hear about us and…"

The cries get louder and Thomas has to raise his voice.

"…no matter how unthreatening we may look we instill fear based on reputation alone. It's pretty ingenious really."

Distracted from what he is saying I look around the room to identify the source of the cries. Thomas simply shakes his head and quickly walks over to a crib on the other side of the basement. I can't believe I didn't notice that before. The other members of the gang groan. One of the gang members,

Eric Roberts, puts his head in his hands and yells across the basement.

"I'm sick of this Thomas. You may think you are the leader but I am the dungeon master and next time we play I'll make you a dwarf with no powers. Not a cool dwarf like Gimly either, he won't ever have a beard or a weapon. Just think about that."

As I ponder what exactly a dungeon master is, Thomas has put the baby over his shoulder and is rocking her back and forth. He pats her back softly and the crying lessens. I'm impressed.

Another gang member, Morris, gingerly raises his hands and looks around to see if anyone else has noticed.

Thomas turns around and angrily growls at the sight of Morris's hand.

"What?"

"I agree."

"Oh put your hand down Morris. My sister works and I like taking care of the kid."

"I'm just saying, last weekend we had a role playing session planned and you didn't even bother to call and say you weren't coming. There was an uneven number, and I think we can all agree on this, it just wasn't the same without you. It hurt my feelings."

Thomas narrows his eyes and looks around at everyone. No one is making eye contact.

"Anyone else feel the same way?"

There is a long pause. No one dares speak a word.

"Well that's just great. Was anyone going to say anything? This bundle of joy is the best thing that has ever happened to me. Isabella here makes me realize I want a family and someday that will take priority. I can't sit around fighting with foam swords the rest of my life. I am ready to grow up and take responsibility for my life."

This is one fight I don't want to get in the middle of. As the silence lingers I wonder if I can slip out without anyone noticing. At this point my dad has to be wondering where I am. I would almost like to see the look on his face to see the scene that is playing out before me. The guys hang their heads. Morris looks particularly forlorn.

"What about foam battleaxes?"

"No."

"Intergalactic death rays?"

"No."

Morris has tears in his eyes.

"Not even plastic light sabers?"

"Damn it Morris, I said no!"

Morris hangs his head and collapses onto the dusty red couch, completely and utterly defeated. The rest of the guys look on in surprise. Thomas softens his eyes and lowers his voice almost to a whisper.

"I'm sorry; I just need to start thinking about my future. I can't do this forever and at some point I will have to move on with my life. Next year I will go off to college and I can't hang around this basement for the rest of my life."

This is getting way too intense for me and I figure it is a good time to leave. I eye the basement steps cautiously and finally rise to my feet.

"Whelp, it is getting late. I really should…"

No one turns to look at me and I figure I can slip out. Thomas, cradling the baby in his arms, looks around the basement.

"I'm leaving the group."

I sit back down. I decide there could be fireworks and I don't want to miss it. The football game can wait. Eric Roberts, quite for the longest time, finally speaks up.

"You are the heart and soul of our group. Do you really want to give up all this now? You have plenty of time to be a grown-up. This is so much fun and we can do anything."

"I'm sorry"

"We need you. You have built an empire here and you are leaving at its peak just to watch it crumble and burn."

The analogy seems a bit of a stretch and quite extreme. The man just wants to do something else. It's not like the world is falling apart. Morris sits up on the couch and looks at Thomas.

"What about Dungeon Wars. We won't have even numbers and we would need someone to take over as dungeon master."

Thomas strokes his chin.

"Eric is a great Dungeon Master and you already have even numbers."

Thomas looks at me followed by the rest of the group. I have a lump in my throat.

"What?"

Despite the pressure I say no. Over the next five minutes the group tries to convince me to join. Thomas gives a long speech on the group's inception and legacy. He goes through a long list of perks including free food, beautiful women, a certain degree of power, and free game play. Half of what he says I have trouble following and the rest of the group looks at each other like it's all lies. When he is done Eric starts in with the brides. He offers me a foam sword, a plastic crown, and a black cape. When I still show reluctance in desperation Eric yells that I can have Morris's sister. Eric immediately apologizes and says she is only hot enough for himself. After verbal sparring between the two separated by long awkward pauses there is nothing left to offer and the group members collapse in chairs around the basement. I don't say anything and Thomas seizes the opportunity. There are tears in his eyes.

"I still love you guys, you have to know that. I'll still be around but…"

His voice trails off. He walks over to the rack of fake swords, picks one out, and walks to the bottom of the basement steps. He takes one last look around the room and leaves. The rest of the group looks so dejected and a twinge of sympathy touches my heart. A group without its leader is like a beast without its head. They both thrash around with no real direction and end up exhausted, disappointed, and hungry. I hesitate and hope I'm making the right decision.

"Hey guys…"

The rest of the group looks up.

"…I think I'll join. I don't understand a lot of the things you guys say and what you actually do but I'm willing to learn."

Eric grabs one of the fake swords off the wall and walks over to me with great majesty. He tells me to kneel before him and puts on a gold crown. Morris jumps up and grabs the sword out of his hand.

"Wait, who put you in charge? I am second in command."

Eric grabs the sword back.

"No, you are second in command but I am his heir apparent."

Morris defiantly crosses his arms

"Okay fine, tell me what that word means and I will gladly give you the sword."

Eric glares at Morris. He pokes a finger into Morris's chest.

"You really think Thomas would want you to be his second in command on the battlefield. You may know strategy but I am the warrior with bulging muscles, a sword broken off in my leg, and am still mowing down enemies wielding the biggest sword you have ever seen. I am definitely the replacement dungeon master and I believe that speaks for itself."

Morris drops the sword and gloomily resumes his seat on the dusty red couch. Eric picks the sword back up and slowly walks over to me, pausing with each step as if to emphasize the importance of what is about to happen. He is humming a grand tune. He waves the sword over my kneeling figure and brings it down onto my left shoulder and then my right. He announces I am now a full and distinguished member of the gang. The rest of the winter and then all through the summer when I come home for vacation I hang with the gang. As it turns out all the rumors about the mischief the gang causes is completely false. They don't crash any weddings or forcibly collect money from different restaurant and retail owners around town. Most nights they have epic sword battles or sit around watching movies. On the weekends there are extensive role-playing games that can last hours and usually continue over several days. They are the nicest guys you could ever hope to meet and being with the gang was so much fun.

When I go back to school in the fall I am the founder and chief organizer of 'Nerd Week'. Every night there are multiple activities for students to take advantage of. A different movie is shown each night and even several classic episodes of the original "Star Trek" T.V. show. One of the actors that played an extra Klingon on the show is the guest of honor. I may have mislead him and told him it was a larger convention event but he signed autographs in full costume and he was a huge hit. The week culminated in a gigantic LAN battle that lasted into the upcoming week. I invite the gang to come down for the culminating weekend and they have a blast.

In case you were wondering the Fearsome Five went their separate ways several years after high school. Several of the members went off to college in different states and it became difficult to get together. Morris is actually married and I know there is a child on the way. The man that sneered at family life and wanted to be a teenager forever now has a family of his own. The group constantly talks about a reunion and getting back together every once and a while to battle but it never quite works out. Eric still lives in Berry's basement and calls me to come over and play with the swords or read comics with him. While everyone else has moved on he still clings to the memories of that basement and the group everyone feared based on pure story. When I sit on my porch as an old man and try to still remember fleeting memories I will think about the day I first entered that basement and the group that once ruled the neighborhood by fear.

THE TATTOO THAT NEARLY TOOK MY LIFE

It seems like everyone has that one worst day that they will never forget. It can be sneaky. You wake up one morning to a beautiful day and your spirits are high. You go to your favorite coffee house to get your usual: an organic blend of rainforest nut and their special house blend. You are listening to your favorite song on the car radio when you reach for your cup of coffee and everything suddenly goes awry. You discover the lid was not secure enough and the hot beverage you love so much spills onto the new pants you just bought. It is all down hill from here. The skies open up and it is the beginning of the worst day you can possibly imagine.

My worst day, of course, starts on a beautiful sunny spring morning. It is my senior year with only about a month of school left. Senior prom is around the corner and I am both nervous and excited. I haven't asked anyone yet but I know the perfect person. I have known her for a couple of years and she truly is a wonder. I tell you dear reader she is gorgeous and may be the girl of my dreams. I have been so close to asking her out on numerous occasions but in the moment of need my confidence falters. This is the day though. It is the perfect opportunity and I would be a fool to pass it up.

This particular morning my sister is driving in to school early to make some final edits to the school yearbook. I hate waking up early so I decide to take the bus. This turns out to be a big mistake. My sister and I make a deal. I get the car after school to drive downtown to theatre practice. I honestly think it will be a good day. The sun is shining and I am actually excited to ask the girl of my dreams to the prom. I'm smiling as I board the bus. I walk past the bus driver, Mr. Kelvin. He is a tall man, at least 6'5". He is massive with the broadest shoulders I have ever seen. He is intimidating in size alone. He has muscles popping out all over his body and realistically he could snap me like a twig if he wanted to. He has a full back tattoo of a skull being impaled by a bloody sword. It is the symbol of the gang he was a member of in high school. I know because when it gets hot he often drives without a shirt on and he loves to tell the story of its origins. I'm pretty sure driving shirtless is against school policy but no one dare say anything.

His head is completely shaved making his features more striking. He has deep scars above his left eye and on his left cheek. No one has any idea where he got them but I imagine it didn't end well for the other guy. On top of everything else he has a really bad temper. I don't really understand why but when he gets really angry his eyes bulge and his pupils become outlined in a faint yellow. He yells and screams at the students and most are afraid of Mr. Kelvin. Every once in a while a student tempts fate. As I board the bus he is already screaming at the students in the back to sit down.

"What the hell are you doing up? Sit down or I will come back there and crack some skulls."

I hunch down in my seat. The man scares me. I view him almost as a ferocious bear that has not had a decent meal in a while and I am his favorite snack. At this point, making eye contact would just anger the beast. The students do not sit down. In fact one of them gets up from his seat, crosses the aisle slyly, and punches another student in the shoulder.

"Oh, I see you Simon. You think you're bad because you punched someone. We didn't punch people in prison. We made sure they couldn't walk for a week."

The kid Simon punched pushes him back. I can see the vein in Mr. Kelvin's head bulge. When the kids notice the set of fierce and piercing eyes staring back at them in the rearview mirror they instantly freeze in place. For a brief moment no one on the bus dares move, preying that maybe the storm will blow over. No such luck. The bus swerves as he turns his head and yells as loud as he can.

"Oh, there is going to be hell to pay. You know I was homeless before I went to prison. You try and scrounge for change and then last through several rounds of homeless boxing. Rich fat cats gather to watch men they recognize from the gutter beat on each other until they can beat on each other no longer. I'm from the streets man."

This particular day I am sitting beside Ryan Phelps. Unfortunately for me he likes to cause a bit of mischief. He looks like an older version of Denise the Menace. He looks at me with a smile.

"Do you have a cat?"

He laughs as if he has made some sort of joke. He is also a little weird.

"Uh, yes I do. She…"

"My mom is always telling the cat to stop scratching the furniture but it doesn't listen. We have lots of chairs that are meaningless but the cat manages to find the most expensive and significant couch in the house. Why do you think that is?"

I have to say I am a cat person. They are so graceful and cute. I find big cats to be absolutely fascinating. They are beautiful and powerful at the same time.

"Hmmm…my cat does the same thing."

"You see the cat knows it is in control. Even though the cat ignores my mother and doesn't stop scratching the couch my mother still feeds it and gives it lots of attention. You get what I am saying."

Yeah, this kid was weird. One day after school I was in the gymnasium practicing for the high school play. After practice I was walking down the hall to leave. I was pretty sure the building was empty except for a few janitors when suddenly I hear someone in one of the classrooms making a lot of noise. Curious I peek my head in. There is a large wooden conference table with empty chairs all around it. At the front of the room stands Ryan in all his glory. He looks triumphant in his pressed khaki pants and stripped polo shirt. He is banging on the podium at the front of the room.

"Come on people. The intergalactic network has to step up in the face of danger. When planets are being destroyed you can't cower in fear. I mean what chance does earth have…"

I look around the room slowly just to make sure there is no one he possibly could be talking to. Just as I am about to say something he turns around. He stares at me in shock as if I just told him the world was going to end. Scratch that, if I told him that he might not be so surprised.

"What are you doing here? This is a closed meeting."

"Meeting? What are you talking about?"

I am confused and sit down in a chair on one side of the table. As I glance over my shoulder I can see Ryan's eyes glaze over. I have done something horribly wrong.

"Stop, you are sitting on Mr. Welches. You are ruining everything. You have to get out of here."

For the record I have no idea what the intergalactic network is but it sounds cool. Yeah, Ryan is crazy but really he is a good kid. He never explains to me what exactly I interrupted that day but he was so adamant that for a second I almost believed him. It was clear that at least he believed it. Sometimes I still wonder if perhaps he isn't so crazy after all. I think about what happened after school that day as I sit next to Ryan on the bus.

"No, I really don't"

"No matter what we do to the bus driver he still has to drive us to school. Sure he can send us to the principle's office but he then has to explain why he let his bus get out of control. We are the ones really in control and it is about time Mr. Kelvin understands it. He is not the one with power."

I frown at him. The bus driver is already in a bad mood.

"Ryan whatever you are going to do please don't. Did you hear him? He cracks skulls. He probably went to prison for cracking skulls. He works on those gigantic arm muscles in preparation to crack skulls. That kid Mark got into an argument with Mr. Kelvin about a month ago and I haven't seen him since. I beg of you…"

Before I can finish Ryan has crumpled up the can of soda he had been drinking, twists his arm back, and chucks it at the bus driver. Doesn't it seem like sometimes the world is going too fast and then other times it slows to a crawl? There is a brief pause as if everyone breathed in at the same time and the can is whizzing through the air in slow motion. I have a split second to think about my fate. I don't want to be known as the kid who died at the hands of the crazy bus driver. The can hits crazy Mr. Kelvin in the back off the head. The bus swerves on to the wrong side of the road before he veers it violently back onto our side of the double yellow lines. Cars blare their horns and Ryan hunches down in his seat. The bus driver stares into the rearview mirror, narrowing his eyebrows. I tell you the look could kill.

"Who the hell was that? No one messes with me and gets away with it. Ever been in a fistfight with a crack whore. I have and she lost."

I shift uneasily in my seat. I try not to look guilty but I think the look of helplessness on my face is giving me away. Mr. Kelvin is the scariest man I have ever met and I am trying real hard not to make eye contact. With a growl Mr. Kelvin pulls the bus over to the side of the road and jumps up from his seat. He saunters down the aisle starring at each of us as he passes. An eerie silence hangs in the air. As gracefully as I can, I nudge Ryan who has his hat pulled down over his eyes.

"Man, you have to give it up. I am too young to die. "

Ryan lifts the hat that is covering his eyes and puts his hand on my shoulder. He has the biggest grin on his face. He whispers so I can barely even hear him.

"Relax. This is thrilling. Live a little, right."

Thrilling? To me this is like a near death experience and let's be honest, death scares me. Many people imagine the grim reaper coming to get them, the dark and shadowy figure with that long stick with a curved blade attached. The grim reaper always has no face, just a black hole covered up by a dark cloak. For me the most terrifying thing I can imagine is the guy that hosted Mr. Rogers Neighborhood coming at me with all the evil in the world. My representation of the goodness and decency of man turned to the dark side sends shivers down my spine. Ryan remains slouched down in the seat and doesn't lift his eyes. I must stop this before something dreadful happens. I lean down in the seat and whisper as softly as I can so Mr. Kelvin doesn't spot me.

"This is scary as hell. Just admit it was you."

"I know you don't understand this but I am on a top secret mission for the intergalactic network."

I push Ryan's hand off me and take off his hat so I can look at him.

"Would you just stop it? You are so full of…"

"Shhhh, they may be monitoring everything we're saying."

NICHOLAS KERESZTURY

"Who is they, what are you talking about."

"For our safety this conversation didn't happen, got it."

"I am getting sick of this crap. The intergalactic network doesn't exist. There is no mission and Mr. Welches does not exist. I am not apologizing any more for sitting on him and I refuse to buy into your warped fantasies."

I expect Ryan to get angry but he doesn't move, starring straight ahead. He whispers out of the side of his mouth.

"Nick, you're a good friend and I have not been fair to you. I have to tell you something very serious. I am a double agent. I am working on the inside, posing as a loyal member of the intergalactic network. I am really a spy for the CIA investigating corruption within the organization."

In that moment I envy Ryan. I don't know if he is telling some semblance of the truth or just plan crazy, but he believes in something grand. His passion is so strong it's intoxicating. I do believe in some of the tall tales. Bigfoot is most definitely real and I've heard the movie Anaconda starring Jennifer Lopez is based on a true story.

"I respect your passion and you may be right but right now I want to live. There is so much I still want to do in my life. The man always looks at me like I killed his cat. For some reason he hates me."

Suddenly I sense a big and threatening force behind me. I slowly turn to see Mr. Kelvin towering over me. I swallow hard. I've heard that for some animals, such as dinosaurs, vision is based on movement. I stop and try to stay absolutely still hoping that he will go away. No such luck. I dare not breath.

"I should have known it was you Nick."

I open my mouth to protest but I don't want to anger the great beast. Mr. Kelvin leans down close to me and lowers his eyes.

"I'm a war veteran, I have seen horrors you couldn't possibly imagine, men driven crazy by the sheer shock of it all. I'll show you those horrors."

I shift uncomfortably in my seat. He continues to stare me down until I am red in the face. I expect him to look away but Mr. Kelvin never flinches or loses focus. His eyes are so dark that all I can see are two black transfixed circles. There is no humanity behind the blackness. I imagine if you stare at them long enough they will take your soul. I am terrified and hot tears start to slowly roll down my cheek. I wipe them away quickly and in a panic choke them back. Mr. Kelvin finally lifts his eyes and looks around the bus. No one moves. He grabs me by the shirt collar and drags me to the front of the bus. He stands back and crosses his arms.

"I want you to apologize to me right now."

I look around the bus at all the other students. No one is out of his or her seat or talking to each other. It seems like everyone in my school is perpetually distracted, never being able to sit still or concentrate on what they are doing. Now everyone is staring straight at me without daring to move. I don't know what to do so I continue to stand there as the silence lingers. I am too shocked to speak. Mr. Kelvin uncrosses his arms and throws his arms up.

"Well?"

"Uh…"

Without warning Mr. Kelvin takes off his shirt and tosses it at me. Some of the students gasp but no one says anything. Wow, his muscles have muscles and for a second my fear is replaced by jealousy. He turns around and shows the tattoo of a detailed skull being impaled by a bloody sword. This was before tattoos became popular and I had never seen one before. The tattoo covers his entire back. It is the best tattoo I have ever seen. The detail is truly remarkable. Both the skull and the sword are in black and white while the blood dripping from the sword is a deep crimson. The mouth is open.

The gritted teeth and faint smile seem to suggest defiance and a certain joy. The eyes are hallowed out with dark lines underneath the eyes and a fainter, smaller line below them. The sword enters the right temple angling down and exits just below the left eye. The blood on the end of the sword drips off it and the droplets fall neatly down the left side of Mr. Kelvin's back, stopping just above his waist. I stare at it open mouthed. Students lean closer to get a better look and the silence is finally broken. A murmur runs around the bus and they all start whispering to each other. Some are horrified while others think it is cool. Mr. Kelvin doesn't turn around. I wonder if he is proud of it and what it means. I stand there staring at it until Mr. Kelvin turns around. There is a glint in his eyes.

"Wow, that is a nice tattoo. It is just so you, really."

He crosses his arms and takes a step towards me.

"Are you mocking me?"

"God no."

"Why do you think I got this?"

I pause. This feels like a test. If I give him the right answer, stroke his ego a little; maybe I can still get out of this.

"Cracking skulls?"

Mr. Kelvin gives me a sideways glance and stares at me without blinking.

"After my parents died I was sent to live in a hole in the wall foster home outside Baltimore. I had to grow up by myself. The only guidance I had was the other hapless orphans. I would have been lost without them and probably dead. We helped each other retain our humanity. This is a symbol of how united we were."

"What does it mean?"

"We live together, we die together."

I don't know what to say. I feel a twinge of sympathy for the man I have feared for many years. Perhaps he is a good and decent man. I walk slowly towards him, overwhelmed with a desire to give him a big hug. He takes a step back suspiciously as I put my arms around me. He pushes me off.

"What I am saying is I am too old for this shit. You…"

He point his finger at me

"…Have been a troublemaker for too long."

I nod.

"If I catch you messing with me again I will…"

He turns around once more and shows me the tattoo. Somehow the skull looks even more menacing. The smile is broader and the blood looks more vivid. I have a dream that night of a flaming skull coming at me in the darkness. It chases me down until I can't stop running anymore and I am engulfed with terror. I finally catch my breath as Mr. Kelvin faces me.

"I am truly beyond sorry."

It is all I could think of to say. Mr. Kelvin turns without a word and sits down in the driver's seat. He turns the key and we continue the ride to school. For the rest of the bus ride no one speaks, afraid to break the silence. Mr. Kelvin constantly stares at me through the rearview mirror. When we arrive at school I slowly get up and walk towards the front of the bus. My heart is pounding so fast I have to clutch my chest to make sure it isn't going to pop out. I keep my head down until I feel a firm hand grab my shoulder. I jump in alarm. It's Mr. Kelvin. I shudder as he turns around a final time to show me the tattoo. There has to be a rule against driving a bus shirtless.

As I walk through the hallway to my locker I am still mulling over what happened. I have never had a bus driver that was totally right in the head. Miss Henrietta Wellington, my elementary school bus driver, always smoked while she drove and cursed at passing motorists. She once told me I wouldn't be so happy when I woke up one day in a card board box I had written 'house' on with magic marker. I can't remember the name of my middle school bus driver although he was kind of cool. On the last day of school he would pull the bus over to the side of the road and play his guitar for everyone. He was a very nice guy and never got agitated with any of the students. I was shocked when he got fired for crashing the bus into the flagpole in front of the school.

He claimed it came out of nowhere and after the bus accident I completely understand. The same principal, Mr. Turnbull, who my dad had punched during the now infamous parent teacher conference, came running out of the school and the two of them got into a huge screaming match. The principal wasn't concerned about the damage to the bus or school property but accused the bus driver of being unpatriotic and anti-American. That was a tough year for Mr. Turnbull. Mr. Kelvin is definitely the craziest I've ever had though. I do wonder if everything he said is true. I am still thinking about it as I walk down the hallway to my locker. As I open it a guy I have not seen around school before comes up beside me and rests his arm against my locker.

"Hey, you want a two liter bottle of soda."

He holds it up for me. My mind is still swirling. I'm really in no position to make decisions and it does sound so refreshing.

"Uh, sure."

I take the bottle and take a big swig. Man, it tastes great. I ask if he wants it back but he says it's a gift. After living in fear and being verbally harassed all morning, it is refreshing to have someone actually be nice to me. I put the rest in my backpack and think nothing of it. The morning passes with out event until my second class of the day. I really like drama class. We don't really do much so it is a great time to just hang out and goof around. There are some unique characters to say the least in our class. Mark, a good friend of mine, is determined to break every record in the Guiness Book of World Records. So far he has been rather unsuccessful but seeing him make his attempts is a great way to pass the time in class. He tried to hold the record for most clothespins stuck to someone's face but he fell short. He looked pretty awesome though. He once nearly ate his weight in cheese doodles but fell several pounds short. I remember that day well. We all cheered him on and bless his heart he was so determined.

He really did inspire me to take risks. Let's be honest, without Mark Solchek I would not be writing this. Unfortunately, for the rest of the class he lay sprawled on the ground with a stomachache. Another guy in the class is Rick. He is one of those guys that writes emotional songs about his inner most feelings and strums on his guitar with great melancholy. His recent emotional song about lost love "Breathing your Essence" is guaranteed to be a hit. Martha is a girl determined to fulfill her dreams as a street performer. She practices different routines trying to find the one that best fits her. One week she decided to be a clown so she went around pieing everyone in the class in the face. In the middle of Mark trying to break the record for the most popsicles eaten in a ten-minute span, my physical education teacher, Mrs. Cooper, bursts into the class. She is attractive in a semi good looking nurse trying to save your life kind of way but I do not understand how she is the physical education teacher. She is so gangly and looks like a penguin that has been shot in the leg when she runs. Following Mrs. Cooper is the assistant principal. It seems like he doesn't want to be here and his ever receding hair line makes him look even less serious.

"I am looking for Nicholas Keresztury. I need him right now."

Everyone looks at me. Crap, what is it now. I am pretty sure I didn't do anything wrong but today is not my day. I raise my hand. Mrs. Cooper walks towards me and I can tell she is pissed. She is relatively young. She has long brown hair she ties up into a bun. She is very thin with what you can tell is a fake tan. She always wears long skirts that taper at the bottom and colorful blouses. I guess you could say the color choices match her personality. She comes over to me and crosses her arms.

"I believe you have something of mine."

What? You have got to be kidding me. Am I going to be blamed again for something I didn't do? What the hell is going on here? I sense some kind of conspiracy.

"I don't know what you are talking about."

"Oh, so you didn't come to my classroom this morning and take what I had sitting on my desk."

"I have no idea…"

I look around me. Mark is sprawled out on the floor clutching his head. The cold of the popsicles has clearly affected him. Rick is sitting in the corner strumming on his guitar. Tears are streaming down his cheeks and he is screaming about some woman named Amy. Martha is moving her hands around her like she is trapped in a box. Her face is painted white and she is wearing a top hat. This week she is working on being a mime. I think she is supposed to not talk but she screams at anyone who gets near her for breaking the box she is trapped in. No one is paying attention so there is no one to come to my aid. What a bunch of weirdoes.

"I know you took my soda."

You have got to be kidding me. That kid did look sketchy and very familiar.

I wonder why he gave the soda to me.

"Some student named Robert reported it."

Oh my god. I knew I recognized him. It's my arch nemesis from elementary school that dated Elizabeth and was always out to get me. He moved to Toledo after sixth grade and I wasn't sure what happened to him. One thing is for sure, he is not going to get. The teacher is saying something but all I can hear are my own thoughts.

"Are you listening? Give that soda back now and I will forget it happened."

Mrs. Cooper holds on securely to my arm as we walk down the hallway to my locker. Some people turn and look but most people don't even notice. As I give her back the bottle of soda she slams my locker shut causing me to jump.

"I am very disappointed in you."

What a day. How many people were going to yell at me today? It's like I cannot

do anything right. A hand grabs my shoulder and wheels me around.

"Hey, buddy. Remember me?"

Damn, its Robert. My old nemesis has come back to torture me once more.

"But, I...I thought you moved away. I remember having a celebration party."

He gives me a sideways glance. The glittery balloons were beautiful and I believe at one point confetti rained from the ceiling.

"Yeah, I know. You posted the pictures online. You looked very happy and the cake saying 'Finally Gone' with a picture of my face on it was a nice touch."

"Okay, you got me. I'm really sorry. Look, let's just put everything behind us."

He laughs.

"I don't care. I just wanted to show you that I am still smarter than you, I will always get the girl over you, I am better than you in every way, and there is absolutely nothing you can do about it."

"But…"

"I'm here to stay and I don't think you'll be forgetting that anytime soon."

"What do you mean?"

"I'll see you around."

The man I called my enemy for so long slowly turns and walks away. I stand there shocked. I spend all day thinking about Kenny and his return.

All the fights and juvenile things we said and did to each other seemed so far away. Weren't we supposed to be adults now? People in High School never seemed that mature though. Some things never change I guess. I wonder if I will ever talk to Kenny after this day or if we might even get into bizarre prank fights like we did as kids. Will things ever change? Will we be old men and still have a love hate relationship that has no end in sight. Maybe we will compete over some classy older woman in the retirement home. I guess time will tell. Right then I just wanted to know how much I would have to deal with him. The school day could not end soon enough and I am relieved when the bell signaling the end of the day rings. Thank god for my agreement with my sister and theatre practice. Theatre practice will be fun and hopefully I can end the day on a positive note. I am also so glad I get the car to drive to practice. There is no way I could get on that bus again today. I would be so nervous and if anything else happened I really would be dead.

The traffic leaving school is terrible. Cars are backed up behind the buses, which haven't left yet. I don't want to be late for practice because I have a plan to ask Mary to the dance. I have meaning been meaning to but this is the day. I look ahead of me to see how long the wait might be. I am growing impatient. I spot a side street directly up ahead but there is one bus in front of me. There is some space between the cars parked on the side of the road and the bus. If I can just get around it I will be home free. I am about to put my foot on the gas but I hesitate. Is it possible I have misjudged the space and not wanting to be late for practice has clouded my judgment? On gut instinct I turn the wheel and round the corner of the bus. I think I have done it when I hear metal scraping against metal and cover my ears. It sounds worse than fingernails on chalkboard. I have hit the side of the bus and it is tearing up the side of my car. I am in a panic. I have no idea what to do. If I get off the road I can figure this all out and maybe no one will notice. I spot a parking spot up ahead and try to pull into it. Unfortunately it is not big enough. I ram right into the parked car. Smoke is coming from the hood of my car. I can't think straight. I have no idea what to do. A crowd is starting to gather around my car.

I slowly get out of the car. The crowd has gathered around. There is some laughing; a lot of finger pointing, and general chatter. Everyone is looking to see what I will do. I spot Kenny in the crowd. He has a gigantic smile on his face. I try and ignore him. I start to tear up a little as I pull out my cell phone to call my mom to see what I should do. As the phone rings I watch a large shadow slowly descend the steps of the bus I just smashed into. The shadow lingers on the bottom of the steps for a moment before emerging into the light. I drop my phone and gasp. It's Mr. Kelvin! I quickly check to make sure I haven't crapped my pants. My heart is pounding so fast I put my hand over my chest to make sure it isn't going to leap out. They say in the face of danger everyone experiences fight or flight, an instinctive response to either run or fight back. I could take one look at him and take off down the street. I wouldn't even look back to see if he was following me, I would just run until I couldn't any longer. I imagine his skull tattoo somehow chasing me down. Conversely, I could run at him with my fists flying. I could go out in one final blaze of glory, taking a heroic stand knowing it might be my final battle. In the end I just stand there. As he looks around him I hope he won't see me. He spots me immediately and saunters over to me.

"Son of a bitch. It's you. You just rammed into my bus."

"What, no…this isn't my car…I think the owner wandered off in that direction. You should go find him and…give him a stern talking to."

He looks me right in the eyes.

"Was it you?"

I want to look away but I can't. His eyes draw me in and I just feel compelled to tell the truth. He is like a human lie detector.

"No, it was…well…"

I weigh my options in my head. I can lie and claim it isn't my car but if he figured it out he would get really upset and possibly kill me. If I tell him the truth he will still be really mad but maybe he will appreciate my honesty and spare my life. As I stare into his eyes a strange sensation comes over me. I couldn't lie to him if I wanted to. It's as if he has some bizarre power over me.

"…yeah it was."

Man, things are not going well. Like when there is a fight in high school and the students gather in a circle around the two kids about to fight, the crowd tightens around us. I want to say something but can't seem to find the words. Mr. Kelvin notices the long scratch along the side of the bus and slowly turns towards me.

"You scratched my bus."

"I believe it is owned by the school district."

Mr. Kelvin scowls. The vein on his forehead pops.

"Are you making fun of me?"

"Oh my god no."

"When I was in the war a fellow soldier accidentally drove a tank into the mess hall. You know what happened to him?"

"Please tell me you didn't kill him."

He narrows his eyes.

"How do you think of me exactly? Everyone else thinks I am a nice and rational guy but you…"

"You make kids cry. Last week Marcus was so afraid after you yelled at him for popping his gum that he wet himself…"

I pause as he continues to glare at me. Is he messing with me? I am now more afraid than ever. He has this weird glint in his eyes that I can't explain. It's not just anger. It is distinctly something else.

"…which is fine. I don't judge."

Mr. Kelvin doesn't react. His deadpan routine is really freaking me out. I really want to know what is happening in that mind of his. Actually, I probably don't.

"Have you seen my tattoo?"

I look around for refuge but all I see are blank faces and nowhere to run. I cover my face with my hands and shake my head back and forth.

"Please, I just want to go home."

"It's not the skull. Here let me show you."

This time Mr. Kelvin starts to pull up his pant leg. I don't know if I can take much more of this.

"I'm sorry. Mr. Kelvin, please…sir…"

The tattoo really is quite beautiful. It is a bright red serpent with green scales entwined around his upper thigh. It's villainous tongue snakes it's way up to his waist. I stare at it in wonder. How many tattoos does this guy have?

"You see this? According to Egyptian lore cobras like this one spend days stalking their prey before they strike. They are the earthly representation of ultimate repentanence, seeking out lost souls who have sinned."

Mr. Kelvin towers over me.

"When the cobra finds its prey it coils around it and squeezes the life out of it."

"But…"

"Let me tell you something, if you are messing with me you are in for a world of hurt. I crack…"

"You crack skulls, I get it. I hit your bus and I'm sorry. My car is smoking and may catch on fire, students are pointing and laughing at me, and Robert will probably pester me about this until I can't take it any longer. Just, back off man."

Mr. Kelvin has a look of surprise flash across his face then quickly narrows his eyes once more.

"Good luck with the car."

I watch him walk away and am in awe. Sure, I am paralyzed by fear but part of me wants to be like him when I grow up. I don't want to be insane or threaten children for a living but he isn't afraid of anything or anyone. He lives by his rules and that sense of independence is so freeing to me. Years later as I contemplate big decisions in my life I often wonder: "what would Mr. Kelvin do?" I sit on the curb and one by one watch the buses take the students home for the day. They all stare at my beat up car as they pass. The car has a ripped gash up the side and a broken taillight. The hood is still smoking. The fragments of the taillight have been cleaned up and I am waiting for the tow truck to come. Man, what an awful day. Luckily my sister decided not to take the bus home so I have someone to keep me company. My sister keeps insisting Mr. Kelvin is a nice man and he was just having a bad day. I keep pleading with her that the man is certifiably insane but she just smirks and says I judge him too harshly. He never yells at her or threatens to crack her skull.

I am angry that he is nicer to her and jealous at the same time. She keeps saying how embarrassing the next day will be when all her friends keep asking her about what happened. That night I dream about Mr. Kelvin turning into a bleeding skull and hunting me down. The skull opens it's mouth wide and is about to swallow me whole when I wake up with a jolt. It was the scariest dream I have ever had. When I fall back asleep I dream of a large cobra slithering into my room with Mr. Kelvin's face for a head. I don't realize until the morning that I have to ride the bus. Mr. Kelvin and I don't make eye contact and for the rest of the school year I don't talk much on rides to and back from school. It isn't until the final day of class that he pulls me aside before I get off the bus for summer vacation.

"Nick, my father was really hard on me when I was a kid. You know why?"

"Uh…"

"Well, part of the reason was I shot him…but he also wanted the best for me. It made me a stronger person. The point is you're a good kid. Don't let other people push you around and live your own life for a change. You might actually be cool if you stand up for yourself. You must think I am a mean old son of a bitch but I care, I really do."

I am overwhelmed with emotion. I hope you don't judge me dear reader but I was truly touched. I will never forget that moment and those words. I still remember them to this day. I had misjudged this guy for so long.

"Thanks Mr. Kelvin. Really, thanks."

I hesitate but slowly put my arm around his shoulder. He gives me an intense stare but doesn't say anything. For some reason the intense stare that once caused a kid to wet himself now seems harmless.

"Alright, you don't have to...let's not make too big a deal out of this...can you get off my damn bus now."

MY LIFE AS A NUT

I am a Halloween baby. I don't mean I was born with fangs or horns. I was born in the early morning on Halloween day. I do wonder what a demon baby would look like though. Would a baby vampire have the innate strength and the thirst for human blood from birth? A mother leans over her precious bundle of joy to change its diaper when suddenly the baby jumps up and bites into her neck. The baby quickly dons a cape and waddles out of the room in search of fresh blood. Instead of breast-feeding a baby the vampire mother gives them bottles of blood or maybe a vampire mother's nipples naturally excrete blood. Or, can you be a werewolf from birth. Sounds like a Disney movie directed by Sam Raimi. I hear the company has been trying to be more edgy.

It would be so kick-ass to see a baby turn into a werewolf, howl at the moon, and attack a nurse. I think the best would have to be a zombie baby. It would waddle around the house half dead and grab at the flesh around your ankles. According to legend if a zombie baby eats enough human brain they became fairly intelligent and can pass as human. They go to school and play outside with all the other kids but they never lose their hunger for human flesh. The hunger becomes overwhelming and then the real terror begins. As my uncle Stan, a proclaimed monster slayer, used to say: "You can attempt to control the very nature of the monster, but you can never quench the hungry of an angry beast."

Then you have those parents that dress their babies as pumpkins or bumblebees and think they look cute. Of course, the baby has no idea what is going on and can't verbalize how humiliated they feel. I've known parents that send out Halloween cards featuring their babies dressed as pumpkins lying among real pumpkins, gourds, and a scare crow. I even knew one parent who put their toddler in a hallowed out pumpkin and had them wear the pumpkin top as a hat. Some parents dress their kids up in goofy costumes well into elementary school and middle school. Come on parents, there is a line for how many times you can put your baby in random things and claim it's cute. One thing I never understood is parents tell their children not to talk to strangers and then one night a year they dress them up as a bunny and show them off to everyone in the neighborhood. It's like the parents who don't chaperone are saying: "Here, take my child. You can be a parent for a while and I'll come pick them up soon, I promise. I need some me time, you understand."

I was born on Halloween night and I was welcomed into the world by a doctor with a Frankenstein mask on. Some images stay with you your entire life and that was definitely one of them. It was burned into my brain and refuses to leave. For the first several weeks I assumed that's how people looked. When I saw my parents I thought they were the weird creatures from another planet. Of course, the doctor that delivered me was apparently a little crazy. He predicted the exact day I would be born and won a boatload of money going to any doctor who could correctly make such a prediction.

It turned out all the doctor's in the hospital were involved in an elaborate gambling ring. His luck ran short, however, when he was fired the day after I was born. He is known for having sex with patients and stealing supplies but by golly he knows how to make a prediction. Okay, so once he was drunk while performing surgery and accidentally left surgical scissors inside a patient but everyone makes mistakes. Did I mention he was wasted when he cut my umbilical cord? It was a miracle he didn't miss and snip my manhood. Not to mention, the chief of medicine lost a lot of money when he gambled on the wrong doctor to be the first to be the correct birthing day. Let's just say he pulled some strings.

Another reason I consider myself a Halloween baby is how important it was in my life. It is by far the coolest holiday ever and the memories from those October 31st long ago will stay with me forever. I think our lives can be defined by the images that stick with us. It could be a photograph, a captured moment in time, or something we witnessed. I have had many of these in my life. I remember my first Christmas, sitting in a baby holder in the middle of the kitchen table. My entire family is surrounding me eating lobster. They are all smiling at me. I actually look really pissed, like I don't understand why they aren't sharing. When I was in first grade I remember having a lemonade stand with my sister and searching for Easter eggs on crutches. It was hard.

When I was ten I distinctly remember begging my mom to take me to see the movie 'Jurassic Park'. I was obsessed with dinosaurs at the time and thought they were so cool. I don't know if I expected a different movie but those dinosaurs were mean and I never imagined them devouring people. I guess everyone has to eat. Now every time I go into the woods at night I swear there is a hungry Velociraptor watching me. I know this is irrational but the fear is deep within me. Some of my best memories come from Halloween though. It was a magical time from childhood when I was given more freedom than usual and was actually allowed to eat as much candy as I wanted. Some of the memories that stick out the most for me were the crazy Halloween costumes I used to wear.

My mom was so creative with her Halloween costumes for me. She would be up all night the night before Halloween to make sure I had the best possible costume. She would spend hours sowing and making sure everything was perfect. She became a permanent resident of the town fabric store. In Kindergarten we wore our costumes to school for the class to see and then we paraded around the school. The cool teachers would hand out candy and chocolate. I was a dragon. Unfortunately, the felt dragon's head extended out and it was very hard to see. I kept walking into doors and accidentally went into the women's bathroom. I was upset when I realized it was twice the size of the guy's bathroom and had a full-length mirror. Even the bathrooms in the academic buildings in college are not equally proportioned. My teacher was crazy and accused me of being a sexual deviant. I had to have a long and awkward conversation with the Assistant Principal about respecting women and their body differences. I had no idea what was going on.

I decided masks were a bad idea. The next year I was a turtle modeled after my favorite stuffed animal named speedy. It was complete with a detailed felt shell and a hat with a flower sticking out of it. It was beautifully crafted but I couldn't sit down unless I removed the shell. Unfortunately, underneath I was only wearing tight green long underwear and a green turtleneck. The shell is also very heavy and uncomfortable and makes me really hot. I stand in the back of the classroom shifting uncomfortably and sweating uncontrollably all morning until I can't take it anymore. I decide to take off the turtle shell and sit down. Once again, I have to go to the Assistant Principal's office to discuss appropriate attire and indecent exposure. I realize now I let an awesome opportunity slip through my fingers. If I was a little older I could have told I didn't understand and she would have to show me an example of indecent exposure.

The crazy costumes continued, until one Halloween I wore an outfit that gotten me into even worse trouble. My mom was super excited and went to great lengths in making me an ear of corn. I wore all black including tight black leggings and a black top. Then, the morning before school started she safety pinned white fabric stuffed with balled cotton all over me to make kernels. On my head I wore a black headband with real corn stalks glued to it. I was so constricted that I felt like a pencil and I couldn't move my body around. I could not bend over and had to remain upright. When kids found out I couldn't get back up when I fell I spent the whole day on the ground being laughed at. I just lay there wriggling and flailing my arms. Every time someone helped me up someone else would push me back down.

It became a fun game for the students at recess. I kept trying to fight back but my arms were constricted too and I couldn't reach out that far. I couldn't even sit down in class. If I tried to sit on a chair I would just slide right off and be on the ground again. I had to stand in the back of the class awkwardly until my knees hurt from standing too long. When I first tried to explain the situation to my teacher she told me I had to take it off or go to detention. I had not learned my lesson and this time had nothing on underneath except superman underwear and that would have been even more embarrassing. When I entered the Assistant Principal's office dressed as an ear of corn she told me to get out and immediately called my mom in for a conference. All I remember is a long drawn out conversation and my mom's tears.

Another reason I loved Halloween is being able to walk around the neighborhood and have the neighbors pass out candy. Getting all that candy and the experience of it all was something I always looked forward to. The first Halloween I was allowed to walk around without my parents I was a tube of toothpaste. Other kids were ghosts, or superheroes, but, once again. I waddled around not being able to move my arms. I looked absolutely ridiculous and I decided right then and there that I was going to design my own costumes from then on and mobility was an absolute necessity. Over the next several years I tried to be as creative as possible with my outfits. One year I was a two-headed monster complete with a red devils outfit and an extra paper-Mache head. It was so badass. I told everyone that I was sent to hell to be the devil's assistant but there was still a part of me that was good and decent. Therefore, I had my real, good head, and the paper-Mache evil head. They were always fighting and bickering with each other. It was the classic good versus evil story.

My favorite costume was the year I went as Macho Ant. I wore all black with an ant mask I designed and black pipe cleaners for antennas. I was a regular sized ant that had been blown up into a gigantic beast ant to fight the anteaters that kept terrorizing the colony. I thought I was the coolest kid ever walking around telling this story to everyone I could find but people just thought I was crazy. They didn't really get that from the all black clothes and the mask made out of plastic berry containers. I probably should have just bought a costume from a store and been done with but I wanted to be creative.

When you are a kid you are so happy running around and eating as much candy as you can get your hands on. It is a time of innocence and I have so many happy memories of running around with my friends from house to house. There is a sense of freedom and rebellion, at least until you get home and your parents inspect the candy. Then, next thing you know half of it is missing and you remember your father has a bit of a sweet tooth. It is really sad when Halloween loses its mystique. When I started high school I still went trick or treating but I wore a cape and told people I was a guy in a cape.

It was still fun but it wasn't as magical as I had remembered. With every passing year the excitement faded. People who gave out candy looked at us funny and some even questioned why we were taking candy away from the kids. The last year I went trick or treating was my sophomore year in high school. I went with my best friend Dan and his sister Kathleen. I was the classic guy in a cape but Dan and his sister were a little more creative. Dan was Popeye, complete with the sailor's outfit and corncob pipe. It was actually pretty awesome. The houses are actually farther apart out where we live so we always drive to different neighborhoods. Dan's sister was older and going to a costume party later so she reluctantly agreed to drive us. She was a half prostitute half vampire. On one side of her she wore tight stretchy pants and a low cut top. On the other side she had half her hair spiked up, pale skin, and vampire teeth. She would first turn the prostitute side of herself to you.

"I've come to suck..."

Then she would turn the vampire half to you.

"...your blood."

Every time she did it she would laugh and say she was going to be the hit of the party. It took me a while to get the joke. She would get mad when people didn't laugh as much as she thought they should. The night was going okay but people didn't greet us with the same enthusiasm they did when we were young trick r' treaters. The thrill of running up to the door and wanting to show off your costume to everyone was gone. The more houses we went to the more I wished for the old days. I looked around at the kids. They were running around smiling, and looking in other kids pumpkin buckets to see what they had gotten. Plus, Kathleen was getting impatient. When we finally decided to go home we hopped in the car and Kathleen punched the gas so she could get us home and go to her party. As she picked up speed Dan's corncob pipe fell out of his mouth and before he could say anything Kathleen ran over it. We went back to check but it was broken to pieces. Dan just stared at it. I will never forget the silhouette of him standing in the moonlight with his hands on his hips.

He crouches on the ground. He runs his hands through the broken remains and sighs heavily. He used the pipe in several plays he was in and carried it around with him most of high school. He called it his good luck charm and never went anywhere without it. He would bring it out during class and pretend he was a world-renowned detective trying to solve the crime of the century with nothing but his wit. I was always his bumbling sidekick. Anytime he went on a date or did something important to him Dan would squeeze it sporadically. He said it gave him confidence. He never went anywhere without it. No one spoke on the car ride home. We knew this was the last time we would go trick r' treating. It was the end of an era and despite the melancholy I smiled at all the great Halloweens I experienced and all the crazy costumes I had worn over the years.

I never dressed up for Halloween after that. The memory always stuck with me and I never really had a good enough reason too. I did wear costumes for plays and dressed as a woman on several occasions but that is a different story. In college, I went to some Halloween parties but never really wore any sort of costume. That was until my first year of graduate school when I decided to go as Mr. Peanut. I am in love with Mr. Peanut. He is just so cool and dapper. He is like an older English gentleman that attends gallant parties and like's to dance the night away, except he's a gigantic nut. Naturally, he is a ladies man and all the upstanding royal lady nuts, I'm thinking Cashew or Macadamia, swoon over him. At formal dinner parties and gallant balls he asks young debutants to dance and they can't help but say yes. He sweeps them off their feet with his dance moves and suave confidence. I hear he even teaches classes on how to be a gentleman. People associate him with class and prestige, but don't let the image fool you.

He is also a bonified badass and likes to live life on the edge. After dinner parties he boards a helicopter and trades in his tux and bowtie for a specially designed jumpsuit and aerodynamic skis. The helicopter drops him onto a steep cliff that's part of the Rocky Mountains and he rides the fresh powder all the way to the bottom. He used to go skydiving until he got bored. He has climbed Mount Everest ten times and if you have ever tried to freeze a peanut you'll find they don't take well to cold weather. It takes a high degree of courage and mental fortitude. Mr. Peanut is so extreme he takes what normal people think is badass and takes it way past crazy. Let's say you go snorkeling on the Great Barrier Reef? To most people this is a very intense experience. People who are more extreme decide to feed killer sharks during sunset.

Mr. Peanut swims naked on the barrier reef with no breathing apparatus. He feeds starving sharks at sunset even though he is bleeding profusely. He carries nothing to protect himself but a small toothpick from a martini he was drinking earlier at the bar where he picked up the most beautiful woman alive. As they charge him Mr. Peanut deflect every flesh craving super shark with a single thrust of the toothpick. He isn't afraid of anything and scoffs in the face of danger. Mr. Peanut also hangs out with the coolest cats in the business. He hobnobs with such stars as Inspector Gadget, Mighty Mouse, Popeye, Bullwinkle, The Smurfs, and Waldo from Where's Waldo. It is so hard to find that guy. Very few people know this but they belong to a secret crime-fighting league constantly saving the planet from super villains such as Shredder, Cruella De Vil, Willie E. Coyote, and Skeletor. In essence, Mr. Peanut has it going on.

I am excited to dress up for Halloween this year and Mr. Peanut is the only logical choice. Unfortunately, I have class on Halloween and we are giving our mid-term presentations. Some friends in the program told me we were allowed to dress up and in the past people wore costumes. I didn't know one person once wore a silly hat and that was it. I had always wanted to dress as my hero Mr. Peanut and thought this was the perfect opportunity. It took me weeks to plan out the costume. I already had a top hat so I bought a cane, white gloves, and looked everywhere and eventually found white shoes. I made several trips to the fabric store buying foam I spray painted a brownish yellow color. It was perfect. I got dressed in my apartment and walked to campus. I got a lot of strange looks, especially when I went into the bakery to buy some coffee. There is an attractive girl behind the counter and I decide if a girl dressed as Mr. Peanut ever flirted with me it would be so awesome and I would be immediately attracted to her.

"So, do you like nuts? If so you can have me."

She looks stunned and I get nervous. My humorous flirtation is lost on her. I realize that may have come off as strange and slightly creepy. Having someone dressed as a gigantic nut come in to order coffee and then start flirting with you would be a little weird. I know I need to take quick action.

"You know, because I'm Mr. Peanut…"

"Actually I am allergic to nuts."

Shoot. I can't tell if she understands that I am trying to be humorous and is flirting with me or simply sharing her medical history. I decide it is best to ask a follow up question to test the waters and get more information.

"Well a peanut is technically a legume and not a nut so you should be okay, but we could always test that theory."

No reaction. I need to really turn on the charm.

"…although, if Mr. Peanut was trying to flirt with you…and I'm not saying he is…he would be more dapper, like hey there lady Cashew you look so good this evening I could just eat you up. If you were a pistachio you would be quite smashing or if you were a chestnut I would say you had nice…uh…anyway, would you be so gracious as to join me at the royal ball."

I decide to just take my coffee and go. I am confused about what just happened and I could tell she was looking uncomfortable. Besides, I need a good pick me up before class. I had stayed up late making the costume and I knew everyone would be so impressed. The class was in the library. I tried to not bring too much attention to myself but as I walked by the older woman at the front desk stopped me. She leans over the desk and whispered because I guess she was concerned people would hear her.

"Sir, I can't let you in."

I look around the room. There is one person sleeping in a chair in the corner of the room. I can't imagine I would be disturbing the peace. I smile.

"Is it because I'm dressed as a nut and there is no food or drink allowed in the library?"

Oh, I am a card but she doesn't seem to get the joke.

"You can't dress like that. This is a place of academic study, not tom foolery."

She stares at me intently. She has shoulder length brown hair tucked up into a bun. There is not a single strand of hair out of place. She is wearing a crisp white buttoned down shirt tucked neatly into a plaid skirt that goes down past her knees. This woman has no sense of modern fashion and needs to live a little. She is also a huge stickler for the rules. I once brought in a bag of cookies to share with the class and she went crazy. She stomped over to me and smacked them out of my hand saying no food or drink was allowed within the library. Like I was in elementary school all over again she confiscated the cookies and put them in a drawer behind the front desk. I imagine when no one was looking she would eat them and giggle to herself. She made sure she confiscated enough food that she didn't have to pay for meals. If I were the real life Mr. Peanut I would sweep her off her feet and whisk her off to climb a mountain with me. As we got to the tallest peak I would kiss her passionately and we would start a torrid love affair. We would live life to the extreme, kicking it up a notch by having bungee sex off the Brooklyn Bridge and making love as the sun sets over Mars. That's right, I am so cool I own Mars and have somehow figured out how to breath on the surface. I am popped out of my daydream when I realize the girl is still staring at me.

"I am going to have to ask you to leave."

There is only one way out of this. I think back to Angus and the first lesson he taught me. If a woman is angry there is one compliment that will get you out of trouble. No matter what she looks like she will appreciate it and immediately forget how angry she was.

"Wow, I really like your shoes."

"Uh, I am sitting behind a desk. You can't even see my feet."

Hmmm, stupid Angus.

"Well, you're the kind of girl who always looks nice so... you know."

I am late as it is and I really have to get to class. This clearly isn't working and if I wait any longer I will be counted absent. She turns for a brief second and I make a break for it. She looks stunned as I run through the library but after a brief pause she takes off after me. I am fast when I want to be but the peanut outfit is cumbersome at best. Despite my years of wearing awkward constricting costumes I never learned to be comfortable in my Halloween outfit. I am waddling like a duck and pushing things out of the way with my cane. My hat falls off but I decide it is too late to go back and get it. It becomes an unfortunate causality.

I try to jump over a chair blocking my path but fall into a display of DVDs. They scatter across the floor and a library employee rushes in to pick them up as I race through the shelves of encyclopedias. Suddenly, on the other end the female librarian appears and I stop dead in my tracks. I turn around but another employee blocks the other end of the aisle. There is nothing I can do now. I hang my head until I find an opening and I am off again. I run past a row of computers and I finally spot my classroom on the far end of the library. All that stands in my way now is a crowd of incoming students on a tour of campus and several tables of refreshments for them to enjoy. So I can't bring a bag of cookies into the library but it's okay to have full tables of goodies. That is hypocrisy and as someone who can't pass up food no matter what it is I am a little offended that no one thought I needed to be fed.

I spot the uptight librarian out of the corner of my eye and with a deep breath I run towards the crowd of students. Some of them look up from their snacks with shocked looks on their faces. As the tour leader discusses how the library is a quiet place of learning and academic study I barge my way through the crowd and accidentally push several people aside. The tour leader screams but is schussed by the incoming students and she squeals in frustration. On my way by I stop for a brief to grab puffed pastries and mini hotdogs wrapped in dough. I can never pass up free food and the pastries are delicious. The classroom is close now and with an extra burst of speed I have finally reached my destination. I yank open the door and shut it hard behind me.

I lean backwards against the door and close my eyes to catch my breath. When I notice the silence I slowly open one eye and then the other. Everyone is looking at me including the teacher, Samantha. No one is dressed up. In fact, no one is wearing a goofy hat or anything Halloween related. I feel duped. The stories of costumes and goofy accessories were a lie. I look at the clock and realize I am five minutes late and someone is standing up ready to give a presentation. I tip toes towards an empty seat at the front of the class and hope no one noticed me come in. Someone begins to laugh and slowly everyone is partaking in the festivities, clapping at my moczy to actually dress up. Loving the moment I take a bow.

"Thank you everyone, you are too kind."

One of my fellow students is clearly not aware of the genius of Mr. Peanut. He looks me up and down and pokes at my foam shell.

"And what are you supposed to be?"

"Can't you tell? I'm Mr. Peanut."

"I thought you were an English butler with a peanut fetish."

I laugh. That kind of makes sense. The teacher just smiles and shakes her head. She is used to my antics. For my first presentation in the program I brought in a life sized cutout of Arnold Swarzenneggar dressed as the terminator. It made perfect sense. A year later I did a PowerPoint presentation featuring a picture of a flaming pumpkin terrorizing a village and an evil pumpkin eating a baby. It was a crowning achievement in my academic career. While I would have been in trouble if I had interrupted a presentation, under the circumstances I have brought some much needed distraction to the stress of presentation day. Everyone loves it until I turn around and show that I did not think about putting a peanut shell in the back. I am wearing way too tight back leggings. Everyone is forced to cover his or her eyes and turn away. I don't notice people's reactions and when I reach down to pick up a pencil I had dropped I give everyone a site no one expected to see. The costume makes it difficult to bend over so I try to get down on my eyes to pick it up and topple over onto the ground. The audible groans turn into laughter. I squirm around until I finally gain my footing and awkwardly rise to my feet only to look down and see my leggings have dropped down to my knees. I quickly pull them up but it is too late. I have mooned the entire class.

There is some laughter but it dies away to silence. I quietly take my seat but the silence lingers. When I sit down the shell gets bumped up above my head so I can't see around it. I could take it off but then I would have nothing on but the leggings and a black turtleneck. It's clear I didn't properly think this through. Finally, the teacher clears her throat and the class begins. As I expected, the presentations are rather boring but the class moves steadily along. It finally gets to my turn and I stand up in front of the class with my full costume on. Luckily my presentation isn't on professionalism and it actually goes pretty well.

Afterwards I go to the bar with several classmates and make a toast to midterms being over. Being Mr. Peanut, I know

I have to order something classy so I go with my favorite drink, an Apple Martini. It's so tasty and I know it is the preferred drink of royalty. People at the bar are dressed up as well. I clink glasses with a girl sitting next to me dressed as a witch. Normally Mr. Peanut wouldn't be seen even conversing with such a disreputable being, but on Halloween I think he can make an exception. Besides, she's pretty cute. As I slowly sip my drink I realize something very important: you have to be able to have some fun once and a while. Sure I embarrassed myself in front of the entire class but I also helped them forget about the stress they were feeling. People always underestimate the power of humor. A good laugh, a chuckle, or even a friendly smile can be a very cleansing experience. After I have had the worst day a good laugh makes everything better. I forget about my worries for a second and am happy. I am someone who wants to make other people laugh and have some fun in his or her life. There are some things I refuse to do like dressing up as a hotdog and getting attacked by a real dog just for laughs, but even then at least I have brought a smile to someone's face.

THE SECRET BEAR SOCIETY

So, I may have participated in a cult. Well, two actually but that just seems crazy. When I think of a cult I think of that crazy group in that Indian Jones movie where they travel to the Temple of Doom. There are human sacrifices and when you anger the gods a man smeared in colored paint rips your beating heart out of your chest. Every time I think about that scene my heart beats faster and I worry somewhere some guy is performing the ritual. I also think about the scene in the new King Kong movie. They literally use the poor girl as a sacrifice to the great ape. With a beast that big and menacing it's almost understandable. I don't think anyone anticipated Kong would fall in love with his meal. I don't suddenly develop strong feelings for the chicken I am about to eat but to each their own. My favorite part was when the girl got up and started dancing and juggling. I understand how Kong felt. If my chicken dinner got up to dance and juggle how in good conscious could I eat it? I'd sign it to a contract and we would travel the country performing a variety act in bars and comedy clubs. I might also go to a big city square, put a hat down, and see how much money I could make before being arrested. Along with sacrifices, I think of weird rituals to appease the gods, including chanting in some ancient language. I always wonder if they are speaking gibberish as an inside joke because no one could really tell the difference

My first experience with a cult involved a blackened bears tooth, an old man I was convinced had come back from the dead, and lots of potato salad. One lazy Sunday in late July I have just returned from swimming in the lake near my house. I am about to officially enter high school and I am trying to squeeze every last bit of fun out of the summer. I grab a Popsicle from the freezer. My dad enters the kitchen and stands at the counter staring at me. I get a sinking feeling I did something horribly wrong. I think about what I possibly could have done. Was it that I drew a mustache and muttonchops in magic marker on my sister's poster of NSYNC lead singer Justin Timberlake? Does he have to be shirtless and showing off his rock hard abs? I guess I'm a little jealous but I think it is rather pompous. It could be the large hole I dug in the yard but I wanted to create a secret underground lair that I could make into a secret hideout. It would be so cool. I ended up sitting in a gigantic dirt hole and cursing that I had ruined my new jeans. When it started pouring down rain I was forced to abandon the hole and the underground lair remains unfinished. My dad clears his throat.

"I hear bears are making a comeback."

My father has this weird glint in his eye and I am not quite sure what he is getting at. I do like bears. My favorite book as a kid was about a family of bears who live in a hallowed out tree and learn profound life lessons. I always thought they were a very misunderstood animal.

"Huh?"

"Mr. Freeman shot one last week."

"Is that legal?"

"Well, he doesn't have a permit but he shoots to live and puts smoked meat in our mailbox every Christmas so I'm okay with it. Boy, did he go too far this time though. He put a couple of bullet holes in the church up on the hill."

"Wait, do you mean Mr. Freeman that lives in the woods? I admire how he is living on the edge."

My dad eyes me suspiciously.

"A church though, really"

Wow, I can't believe it. Yeah, old man Freeman is crazy but may be one the coolest men alive. He got tired of living a cushy life so he decided he would live in the woods as a rugged pioneer. He sold all his possessions including his house and put all the money into a bank account just in case of emergencies. He never married and doesn't have any children. He bought a shack in the woods behind the church on the top of the hill. He still went to church every Sunday and still occasionally went into town to pick up supplies. After a year or two he decided he was still leading too blessed a life and abandoned the shack for a quiet cave deeper into the woods. He grew a gigantic mountain man beard and started wearing brown leather hiking boots. He raided the local Army Navy store, buying everything from cooking pots to a wide variety of survival knives. For further protection from wild animals and for hunting he bought a shotgun with all the ammo he would ever need.

No one has seen him for at least several years. I wonder why old man freeman left his cave and how he ended up at the church. Later, I find out a black bear wandered into his cave in the middle of the night looking for a place to sleep. Old man freeman wakes up to the bear growling over him and before he can react the bear clawed him across his face and chest. In a panic freeman grabbed his shotgun but it was so dark all he could see was a dark mass standing over him. He didn't have time to think and shot wildly. The bear stood on its hind leg and let out a ferocious growl before running out of the cave and into the night. Old man freeman breathes a sigh of relief and touches the deep gash over his eyes. A sudden wave of anger and adrenaline surges through him. He jumps to his feet but the stabbing pain makes him grab his chest. Ignoring the pain and the blood dripping in his eyes he tracks the bear the several miles to the church.

He has hunted all kinds of animals in the surrounding area but he has never been able to get close enough to a bear to hunt it and they scare him. The sound of organ music from the Saturday night service can be heard as freeman cocks his shotgun and shoots at the bear as it passes the front entrance. He misses. The organ music stops and shocked chatter can be heard. When the priest exits the church to see what is happening he sees a second shot and a third enter the side of the church. Unfortunately, the bear gets away and an overwhelmed Mr. Freeman collapses onto the grass. He drifts in and out of consciousness as an ambulance is called and he is rushed to the hospital. He hasn't left the wilderness that surrounds the cave in years and the hustle and bustle, bright lights, and general ciaos of civilization seems foreign to him. In an ironic twist the church is pays for all his medical bills and hopes he once again becomes a member of their church. Many of the members are hoping they can save him from a lifestyle that they don't quite understand. You have to admire Freeman though. He is a modern day badass.

"You have to admit that he is so rugged and cool. He is out there doing his thing and not caring what people think. I am here in air-conditioned cushiness and he is living on the edge of extreme man. He runs to the edge and jumps, excited to face the consequences. The man is a legend.

My dad crosses his arms.

"Legend, huh. Well, if you call a man who went to a place of worship and shot it up like he was in an action movie a legend then yes..."

"Well, a lot of the hero's in my dreams are fighting wild animals, mostly with sticks, but…"

My dad looks at me funny and raises his eyebrows.

"Is that normal?"

I pause.

"I don't know. Anyway, if I shot up a church would you still love me?"

My dad doesn't say anything at first. He goes to the fridge, takes out a beer, and twists off the cap.

"Well, I would be very disappointed. That's not how I raised you."

"But if I did…"

"What denomination?"

My dad's stance on religion is confusing to me and I would assume it would be wrong no matter what denomination it was. Further, would my dad respond differently if I shot up a gas station or an office building rather than a church? If it was a church would I get a harsher judgment in court? Man, these questions are deep. Plato would be proud.

"Uh, does the denomination really…"

"I am just trying to get a clear picture here. I don't feel comfortable with this. Go ask your mother. Whatever she says I agree with."

"Okay, but shouldn't the answer automatically be yes."

"Damnit, I don't know. You ever run through the woods shooting at a bear and put three bullet holes in a church then I will answer your question."

"Aha, but what if your answer influences whether or not I do fire a gun at a church."

"What?"

"Okay, so let's assume I believe I have no choice but to fire at a church…you know, to save lives or something…"

175

My dad frowns.

"I am not playing this game."

"…Just listen. If I know you will still love me I might be more likely to pull the trigger and if not I might be less likely."

"Or maybe you should never shoot up a church. There, problem solved."

"So…"

My dad grits his teeth and widens his eyes. I decide to let it go. The question did seem out of place and now the conversation has turned sour. My dad takes another swig of beer and leans against the kitchen counter. I shift my weight nervously and look out the window. I decide to change the subject.

"So, how did he end up shooting…?"

"The bear ran in front of the church and Mr. Freeman got a little excited. You're missing the point. Bears are back and goddamnit, I'm excited."

I have no idea why he is so excited. He giggles like a school girl when he talks about his naked philosophy group but that's about it. Something else must be going on here. Man, only in West Virginia could this happen. People are obsessed with hunting. I remember we took a month long hunter safety course in middle school where everyone practiced shooting rifles. Talk about a lawsuit waiting to happen. I had trouble hitting the targets and gained the unfortunate nickname of Buckshot. I've seen older men sitting on their porch with a rifle in their lap. It keeps away annoying children, door-to-door salesmen, babies, mailmen who insist on knocking on the door to say Hi, and deer trying to eat the flowers. It's pretty genius actually. It ensures privacy and the status as the neighborhood grumpy old man. My dad continues to stare at me.

"So, wanna come to a picnic."

"If there is food I am there."

My dad smiles as if he is plotting something.

"Oh I wouldn't worry about that. With your adventurous palette you should be fine."

I will literally go anywhere and do anything for food, the stranger and more exotic the better. One of my heroes is Andrew Zimmer. He travels the world exploring other cultures and eating all the native dishes. He has eaten weird things like bird nest soup, grilled insects, jellyfish, and bull's testicles. People used to ask me what my dream job was and I always mentioned being paid to visit other cultures and eat their food. I would call myself the world's finest culinary anthropologist. In case you wonder I am nowhere in the league of Sir Andrew Zimmer but I have eaten some bizarre stuff. In Mexico I ate cow brain and have to say it was very good. The texture was weird but it had a lot of flavor. I've eaten snail and I liked it a lot as well. When I was camping with the boyscouts we ran out of food so we ate crawdads out of a stream. They were okay but not filling at all. My weirdest experience with food happened on a trip to China. I first ate an egg that had been buried in the ground for a month. The Chinese call it a 1,000-year-old egg. It is a delicacy and I assumed it wasn't going to be as bad as I imagined. Unfortunately it was worse and tasted like an egg that had been sitting out for a month. I also ate grilled grubs on a stick but I don't like to talk about it. While I had a few bad experiences in China I still pride myself on the fact that I will try anything once. Eating bizarre foods lets me channel my adventurous side and makes me feel like a badass.

I decide I might as well attend. It sounds fun although my dad is a little too excited. His smile is unnerving, like he knows something I don't. I have no idea what to expect but I am guessing it has something to do with bears. It is a beautiful day. I walk past the old church leading to the grassy meadow on the top of the hill. There are two tables spread with all the traditional picnic items: burgers, hotdogs, potato salad, brownies, and homemade lemonade. The star of the meal, however, is bear meat. It has been slow cooked in a tomato-based sauce until it is tender. There is a small crowd of people there including several neighbors. I had no idea this was such a popular event and so far it is just your average picnic. All the food is delicious and everyone is in good spirits. One of the neighborhood boys is flying a kite and the sunshine feels great.

I have never tried Bear meat and when it is finally time to eat I bite into the juicy morsel. It has a very gamey flavor, similar in taste to deer meat. It is a little tough, and fattier than I expected. After everyone has eaten his or her fill we all gather in a tight circle in front of the church. I am not really sure what is going on and the wait seems to go on forever. I wonder if this is going to be a prayer of some sort. Someone comes out of the church and starts walking towards the circle. He is a short, very thin older man with wispy white hair. He is quite frail and uses a cane to walk. The best word I can use to describe him is withered and I really want to know how old he is. He is wearing a blue robe that extends down to his ankles with a rope the ties around the waist. A golden necklace with what looks like a blackened claw attached dangles from his neck. As he approaches some people in the circle bow their heads in respect. I stand there confused. Did I unknowingly stumble into some kind of religious ceremony?

"What is going on?" I whisper to my dad standing next to me, "This guy looks like he should be dead."

Several people in the circle turn to stare at me, including the old man himself whom by this time has reached the center of the circle. I need to work on my whispering. The old man walks up to me and places his hand on my shoulder.

"Be gentle my son."

A shiver runs down my spine. His hands are very cold. He smiles and takes his place in the middle of the circle. He requests that everyone hold hands and close their eyes. I still have no idea what is happening but I close my eyes and feel the light breeze on my face.

"We all have a special connection with nature and must respect it. I want you to seek out your own special connection and live in harmony with the creatures of the forest. 100 years ago the forests around this church were filled with black bears..."

Is he saying he was alive 100 years ago to personally witness this? I knew it. How has he managed to escape death all these years? Maybe he has a secret to long life and will never die but just get older and older looking until he shrivels up.

"...50 years ago the population slowly began to decrease with the development of the area. Their numbers have dwindled over the years until today there are very few left."

The old man raises his arms to the sky and tilts his head back. His blue robe waves in the breeze.

"We ask you gods above to bless the land and bring back the animals that once roamed the hilltops. Everyone open your eyes."

I look around the circle. It seems like I am the only one confused. I want to go along with everything but I'm trying to figure out what just happened. I learn later that we were not preying but sending an appeal to the bear spirits. We want the spirits of the bears that were once prominent to come back and repopulate the area. I look around the circle. People are really into this. The old man gestures towards the church.

"We have a special guest with us today."

The sun momentarily blinds me, but when I look again into the circle steps old man Freeman. People gasp. The claw

179

marks on his face have been stitched up and bandaged. He is wearing his signature leather boots and has a large knife held in a sheath by his side. I am absolutely shocked. If I wouldn't be so heavily judged I would clap my hands giggling and ask for his autograph. His voice is deep and rough.

"I could be mad about what happened to me, but…"

I can no longer contain my excitement.

"I'm sorry, did you really kill a mountain lion with your bare hands?"

Old man Freeman eyes me suspiciously.

"No actually. I always use my shotgun. Now…"

"Wow, that's so awesome. If you live in the wilderness though how do you bathe?"

My dad nudges me so I will stop talking but these are important questions that must be answered.

"Well…"

"What have you shot? "

My dad nudges me harder. He whispers in my ear continuing to look down.

"Seriously, let it go."

Mr. Freeman sighs and I decide that is enough questions for now. After giving me a long look he continues.

"Well, I am here for the ceremony. The bear that attacked me proves they are coming back to the area. What we are doing here today makes a difference. It is time to kiss the tooth."

Kiss the What? I am confused. The old man gestures at the sky and takes off his necklace. I think things couldn't get any crazier when I am passed the blackened thing that was around the old man's neck. I have no idea what to do with it. I hold it in my hands and suddenly realize what I thought was a claw is in fact a bears tooth. What the hell? I look up to see the old man starring at me.

"You must scratch yourself with the tooth until you draw blood. We keep it in veils inside the church to document your sacrifice."

I knew this was some kind of cult. I am horrified. My lips curl and I put my head in my hands. I want to run but my legs buckle and I can't seem to move. The old man lets out a soft laugh and follows it with a dry wheeze. He coughs for some time before catching his breath.

"I'm kidding. The look on your face was great. Oh, what a card I am. Relax, no blood will be spilt...this day."

I mull his comment over in my mind. I notice he emphasized "this day" and am suddenly glad there are witnesses.

"Good one."

"You need to kiss the tooth."

Everyone is looking at me.

"Uh, what?"

"You need to kiss it to bring back the bears. Their spirit inhabits the tooth."

I make a face and the old man frowns. I look down at it. I wonder if it started out blackened and how many people have kissed it. It's possible that it is washed every time but would that wash away the spirits. I make another face and the old man crosses his arms.

"Well?"

"Is it sanitary? If I kiss it isn't that like kissing everyone in the circle."

My dad nudges me in the side.

"Just do it," he whispers.

"The man kissed it and probably breathed his old man breathe all over it. He smells like death. I doubt the bears would know."

The old man crosses his arms.

"I am standing right here. Please, you are angering the bear gods. They can hear you."

"That is ridiculous…"

My dad throws his arms in the air.

"Would you just kiss the damn tooth! I understand this is one big joke and no one takes this seriously but it's meant to be fun."

Both Mr. Freeman and the Rip Van Winkle look-a-like glare at my father. They clearly think this is serious business but they don't say anything. I don't want to argue. I hold the tooth in my hands and turn it over to the side I think is more sanitary. I close my eyes and bring it closer to my mouth. The tension hangs in the air as people look on in silence. I give the tooth a slight peck and toss it to the next person. After everyone kisses the tooth we do some final chanting to finish the ceremony. As the circle breaks I spot old man Freeman walking towards the church. I run after him. He stops in front of the bullet holes in the church door and runs his fingers along the blackened edges. I walk up behind him and put my hand on his shoulder. He jumps and instinctively puts a hand on his shotgun.

"Mr. Freeman I have to say I am a big fan. You are one of my heroes."

"Oh common kid, I'm nobody's hero."

"You survived a bear attack though. You starred death in the face and that bear could have killed you."

Old man freeman touches the deep gashes on his face and frowns. I cringe and look away.

"I'm sorry. It's a pretty kick-ass scar though."

"Yeah, I guess."

"So, I was wondering if I could be your cool sidekick. I have been working out recently. If I saw a bear I could totally rip it apart. I was thinking though, I don't think a shotgun is a good fit for me. Perhaps I could get a mini-gun or a grenade launcher."

Old man freeman puts his hands on his hips and looks up at the sky. I thought he would be more excited.

"Look kid, I almost shot up a church congregation. I left society to deal with my pain and I have done that. I'm retiring."

"What…you can't retire. I need to know your ass kicking ways. I need to find my own cave and live for myself. You know, find my inner strength."

Mr. Freeman doesn't react.

"You have family, right?"

"Well, Yeah."

"I suggest you learn to appreciate it. That will make you cool in my book."

Mr. Freeman turns around and walks across the clearing into the woods. I don't care what anyone says, he is still the ultimate badass. He keeps true to his word about retiring. He builds a modest house on the edge of the clearing and is now a proud member of the church congregation. He now bathes but he kept the beard and it is a reminder of the time he spent as a mountain man. When he misses his former life he sleeps in his cave but makes sure to block the entrance so a bear can't stumble upon him in the middle of the night. When he is lonely he falls asleep clutching his shotgun. Heaven help anyone who enters his house late at night. He even started dating a woman working at the local video store. Every time I go to rent a video she feels the need to mention how passionate it is having sex with a mountain man. After old man Freeman leaves I sit on the church steps. I still admire the man. I can't imagine what he has been through but he dealt with his issues and he is a better person for it. More power to him I say. The old man who led the bear ceremony walks over to me.

"The gods thank you. Here's your card."

I suddenly notice a necklace draped around his neck. It has a bears tooth in the middle with beads and feathers on the side. Was he wearing that before?

"Is that the same bears tooth that you…"

"Yes."

"The one we all kissed?"

"Yes, it is."

"Do you wear that all year long?"

"I only wear it for this special ceremony. It's symbolic. I'm really glad you came."

He looks at me with concern in his eyes. I can tell he really cares about what he is doing. Maybe he really does believe the bears will come back and become a more significant part of the environment. I am still not sure why that is so good but it would be cool. As I look at him I can't help but feel touched by the old man. He is like that lovable older gentleman in the park playing checkers with himself. Sure he may be crazy, but he is loving and always sees the good in everything.

"Son, I know this all seems very strange but we just want the bears to come back and become a part of the community again. We all have a strong connection to the nature we see around us whether we see it or not."

"I guess."

I watch him walk away and then look down at the card. It is yellow with a picture of a bear on it. The bear is stenciled in black pencil and the bear has a huge toothy grin. Next to the bear it says "congratulations, you are now a proud member of the Forks of Cheat bear society." This has to be a joke. Really, there is such a thing as a bear society. It does make it sound like some kind of cult. I imagine people living in homemade shacks in the woods. Every morning they eat beans out of a kettle and reminisce about the good old days when the bears were the kings of the forest. Three times a day they worship the bear gods and chant to them hoping they will come back to save mankind. I still have the card in my wallet and now can say I am indeed a proud member of the bear society.

It has come in handy in the past. About a year ago I was back in town for Christmas break and was getting a hair cut from a local barber I have never been to before. When I went to pay I opened my wallet and he saw the card. He has been part of the society since he was a kid, fondly remembers the rituals, and says it was a big part of his childhood. I was shocked he knew anything about it, it had been taking place for so long, and even more shocked when he didn't charge me for the haircut. Maybe being part of a cult has its benefits. From then on anytime I go to a local business around time I bring out the card in hopes I will get stuff for free. No such luck. Everyone looks at me like I am crazy when I ask if they are a member of the bear society but I will keep trying. I am now very glad I attended what I thought was a simple picnic.

MARDUK, MURDERER OF CHILDREN

My second brush with a cult like experience happens has happened at my house the past five years. On a chilly morning in late December the peer pressure is getting to me. People look on with expectation and shout words of encouragement. I wonder if I am trying to prove something to myself. If I do this will I somehow prove that I am ready to face my fears and conquer anything that stands in my way? I take a shot of whiskey and feel the slow burn as it slides down my throat and warms my belly. To my left a neighborhood kid, who has already done it three times, smiles slyly. To my right my girlfriend stands in anticipation. I suddenly realize the girl I love is meeting my family for the first time and I stand shirtless and barefoot in front of a group of drunken onlookers chanting my name. What must she be thinking? I take a deep breath a walk quickly across the bed of hot coals. I have completed the traditional fire walk and I feel great. It makes me wonder what else I can accomplish.

The scenario I just described happened several years ago. My dad is a member of a self-titled freethinking group. It is primarily made up of agnostics, people who do not like the idea of organized religion, and atheists, people who do not believe in god altogether. The group also includes members that aren't particularly concerned with religion but like to have discussions on the matter and other philosophical issues. The group is really open to anyone and members are encouraged to freely discuss what interests them. The group is mainly made up of the members of the Naked Philosophy Group, (The Big Bad NPG as I now call them), plus one woman. The male members of the Big Bad NPG are smitten with her and are not really sure how to act around her.

For the past five years the group has sponsored a winter solstice party, a party organized to take place on the shortest day of the year and traditionally was done to appease the sun god to bring back the sun. Winter Solstice was a ritual conducted by the early Europeans and can be traced as far back as the mesopatamiums. As the Winter Solstice approached, with its long cold nights and short days, many people feared the sun would not return. Special rituals and celebrations were held to welcome back the sun. It is also a celebration of the beginning of winter. The party, coinciding with the solstice, takes place every year on December 22nd. We don't take it as seriously as the early Europeans and it is really just a great excuse to have a kick-ass party. The food is great, friends gather to have a good time, everyone enjoys great wine, and the merriment overflowith. When they needed a more private house with the ability to build a bonfire and full access to the night sky my family volunteered to host.

There was great anticipation before the first solstice party and I had no idea what to expect. We thought there would be a small crowd of family and friends but over 50 people came. Over the next couple of years strong word of mouth would create a buzz within the community and this past year over 100 people showed up. The food for the solstice party is traditional pagan food so people bring soup, bread, and fine cheeses. It is all very delicious and there are never any leftovers. As with any great party there is also all the alcohol you can drink. The key beverage is whiskey, playing a key role in the headlining event of the evening.

I've heard next year Uncle Wally is bringing moonshine. He makes his own special brand, brewed in his bathtub. The stuff is fierce and could double as gasoline. Days afterwards there is lots of left over alcohol and there is still cold beer months later. The party is great every year but the craziest one happened two years ago. I had been dating Kristin for several months. I had told her about the event and she was intrigued. She had not met my parents yet and I knew taking her would be like throwing her into the lion's den. Most guys introduce their girlfriends to the family during a break from school or work and when the family can sit down and get to know her but that's boring.

I decided if she had a good time and could accept the overwhelming strangeness of the Winter Solstice Party it was a sign I had met someone special. Truth be told, I was in love and was waiting for the best time to tell her. I had no concrete plans for when and where but if things went well I thought this would be a perfect place and might be romantic. With the flames of the bonfire rising high in the air behind us I would hug her close and tell her I loved her. It would be the perfect moment, a grand story you tell people when they ask how you met. Of course there is the concern things could go horribly wrong and she would push me into the fire instead of say it back but it is a risk I was willing to take. The first year of the party I brought my ex-girlfriend and it went poorly. She was highly religious and people in attendance made her uncomfortable. She also protested to some of the traditions that were to be established. Late in the evening everyone gathered around the fire to chant to Marduke, an ancient god worshiped by the early Mesopotamians. During the chanting her lips curl into a scowl and she crosses her arms. People should probably be running at this point but they don't know any better. After the chanting she looks around at everyone and blurts out:

"How dare you worship him? He murders and eats children!"

It's strange that she speaks about him in the present tense, like he is going to pop out from behind the bushes at any moment and go on a bloody and murderous rampage. There is a small pause as everyone stares at her and then back at my dad. People became nervous and a murmur runs through the people gathered around the fire. Some demand to know more about the god they were trying to appease. My dad tried to reassure everyone this was not true and shouldn't be taken so seriously.

"No, it's not true. People please, he's a loving and gentle… alright I don't really know much about him, but…"

There was some yelling and screams of discontent. Some people got upset and stomped off towards the house but most people stuck around, ignoring the claim. My ex-girlfriend grabs my arm and starts to march me away.

"Come on Nick, let's go."

I was embarrassed when I learned she was lying and soon realized she was literally crazy and mean to those that didn't share her beliefs. The relationship ended soon afterwards. In truth, the origins of Marduk are fascinating. Even though the Mesopotamians worshiped multiple gods, Marduk was their chief god. They believed as winter approached he would do battle with the monsters of chaos in an epic battle to save the sun from extinction. If Marduk failed and the monsters of chaos prevailed the sun would shrivel up and die. I think this is awesome. I try and imagine what the monsters of chaos look like. Do they have gigantic horns and spiked tails? Perhaps they have razor sharp teeth designed to rip you apart. In my mind they are simply a cloud of blackness, a swirling mass of absolute evil.

In my mind, Marduk looks like Arnold Swarzeenegger, before he became the governor of California of course. He looks like Arnie when he was a world champion body builder and killing over fifteen officers at a police station in Bakersfield. Even his muscles have muscles and he carries the weight of the universe on his shoulders. He has the additional strength of every person on the planet pulsing through him. He stands heroically between the dark mass and the sun, equipped with the best of modern weaponry. He has a rocket launcher with a sleeve of rockets slung over his shoulder. He has automatic machine guns with unlimited ammo, multiple mini-guns, and double-barreled shotguns. He also has enough explosives to blow up the sun and destroy it all on his own but he knows how to use them. He is the ultimate badass.

According to tradition, at the solstice every year the Mesopotamia king would travel to the temple of Madre and swear his allegiance to the one true god. He was supposed to die and return to Marduk to fight by his side. In reality Marduk doesn't need any sidekicks and has been kicking ass and taking no prisoners for centuries but he appreciates the sign of good will. The Mesopotamians, however, don't want to have to find a new king every year. Once a king is elected he rules until his death. The Mesopotamians used a "mock" king instead. They dressed a criminal in the king's clothing and brought him to the winter solstice celebration to represent the king. For a night he was given the same rights and privileges as the real king.

It was said to be an honor for the criminal, an unselfish act that would absolve his sins and get him a seat in god's kingdom. Then again Marduk might be angry when he finds out he was tricked. At the end of the celebration the "mock" king is stripped of his royal clothes and slain, sparing the life of the real king. Perhaps he is too distracted battling the monsters of chaos, but Marduk never knows the difference and the sun continues to shine year after year. We do not sacrifice a criminal at our celebration. It would probably damper the mood. It is not nearly that serious and a great party.

When I told Kristin about Marduk she also thought he was a badass. She imagined him more as Chuck Norris with his superior martial arts skills. As we turn onto my road and head down the driveway leading to my house I look over at Kristin. She is so beautiful. I am excited and nervous at the same time. It snowed the night before and there is a fresh layer of snow on the ground. My parents thought it would affect the turnout but people still showed up in abundance. I introduce Rebecca to the quests at the party including my parents and I make sure I try all the soup that people have brought. So far things are going well. After the fire has dwindled some we go out to the fire to begin our ritual.

My dad is leading the festivities but I don't see him. I turn around and spot him coming out of the basement. He is stumbling everywhere and runs straight into a pine tree on the side of the house. Someone has to run to his aid and untangle him. Oh my god, he is drunk. I realize this could be bad. My dad doesn't drink often and it is usually with Berry, a friend of his. As a kid I used to go to sporting events with them. Berry always heckled the security guards and threw peanuts at them. On one occasion, he kept throwing them at two female security guards turned around standing at a railing several rows down. Wrongly, the security guards removed from the stadium a rowdy group of college students seated behind us.

Luckily I was not there, but once at a Florida State college game he ran onto the field wearing only a tight flesh colored body suit. He is quite fast and no one was able to catch him. Finally the Florida State mascot, a painted Native American warrior riding a horse, chased him down and tackled him. People thought it hilarious and the game was delayed. It was a televised game and all the sports shows had a field day showing what happened over and over again. Watching SportsCenter the next morning and seeing the replay of the event was awesome. Berry called it the best night in jail he had ever spent.

As my dad starts to walk over, stumbling all over himself, I notice he is wearing a red hat on his head. As he gets closer I recognize it from a recent beach trip. It is a crab hat with long red claws coming out of the top and large googoly eyes on the front. It is the most ridiculous thing I have ever seen and I assume anyone who ventures out in public wearing will be instantly arrested for violation of human decency. I half expect police offices to storm the scene. The fire blazes behind him and for a while he just stands there. The crowd gathered around the fire look around nervously. He looks into the fire and his eyes grow wide.

"Just to clarify, I am not the devil."

As he says this my dad falls over into the snow. He tries to pull himself up but tumbles backwards over a chair. When he gets up the red crab hat is covered in snow.

"See, I'm a fallen angel."

He chuckles as if he has made the funniest joke in the world. He frowns when no one else laughs. I look at Rebecca. She looks confused. I am not sure what she was expecting but

I am guessing this was not it. My dad wobbles towards the fire with a gleam in his eyes.

"I am going to walk first everyone."

My mom saves the day, steering him away from the fire to make sure he doesn't fall in. He sits in a chair next to the fire to sober up. From his chair my dad passes around sheets of paper with the words people should chant in unison in order to bring back the sun. Of course we are chanting to Marduk but we are also chanting to a new god named Angus. Angus is actually a Celtic god. He is the god of youth, love, and beauty. He had a harp that made irresistible music, and his kisses turned into birds that carried messages of love. These messages travel throughout the countryside bringing good luck to all. If someone has sinned they must travel to his underground fairy palace to seek salvation. If they admit their sins and complete a series of trials and tribulations to prove their worth they are saved and returned as a changed person. When the sun disappears and the days get long Angus sends his love to the people to stay strong when the darkness becomes overwhelming. Oh, common. Marduk is so much cooler. The god I choose to worship manifests himself as Chuck Norris kicking ass and taking names. Nothing stands in his way and he stamps out evil anytime and anywhere. He looks like Arnold Swarzennegar and is unfazed by the attacks by the monsters of chaos. He has every weapon known to man and shows no fear.

If Marduk is a mix between Chuck Norris and Arnold, Angus is the Meg Ryan of gods. He is gentle and you can't help but fall in love with his kindness. Love torn softies go crazy over him. He is painfully plain looking but people continue to claim he is beautiful despite evidence to the contrary. Yes, he may be cute but he is so annoying he stopped making movies in the mid nineties. Angus plays a harp while Marduk rocks the electric guitar. I've always wondered why angels play harps. I think they should increase their repertoire. With the Invention of IPODs people are able to personalize their music choices and have it all at their fingertips.

When angels appear to someone they could appear with the person's favorite music in the background. I'd be convinced. I wonder if I learned to play the harp women would flock to me. I would probably just attract unicorns and half men half horse little people that play lutes. They also have those tiny elf ears and sing like angels. Then again, if I rode up to a woman riding a unicorn and playing a lute, those little creatures are great teachers, I might get a date. Anytime you are trying to flirt with a girl and it is not going well, playing a lute makes it okay. Realistically, Marduk and Angus make the perfect team, kicking ass and spreading love and hope to the people.

After the chanting my old babysitter, Rachel, begins the fire dancing. I have so many great memories. She was my babysitter when I was four up until I was in my adolescence. I remember her chasing me around the house when I was going through my naked phase. I found clothes so restricting even though the neighbors disagreed. I also remember picking blackberries in the light rain. We made jam with it and it was so good. Of course we made so much of it I had to find a way to incorporate it into every meal: making pies, tarts, smoothies, frozen desserts, and even putting them in omelets. I tried making blackberry wine in the bathtub by combining juice and vodka but it tasted funny and when I was stirring it I accidentally fell in. My mom thought I had a major allergic reaction and immediately called the Center for Disease Control when she saw my purple skin. I was also worried when I picked blackberries and ate them in early October. Superstition in the United Kingdom holds that blackberries should not be picked after September 29th as the devil has claimed them, having left a mark on the leaves by urinating on them. They were tasty and it was so worth it.

Man, Rachel is a really good fire dancer. She has two balls on the end of chains that are lit on fire. She twirls them around her body and through her legs. She is twirling them so fast they start to look like speeding lines of fire. It is beautiful and breathtaking. It would be so awesome to learn. Out of the corner of my eye I see my dad stumbling towards the twirling fire. I immediately think of what could happen. I imagine him stumbling and accidentally catching himself on fire as he stumbles around in the cold. It would create the same chaotic scene as when my dad burned down the Indian camp. Luckily, he stops just before he reaches the twirling fire and stands with his mouth agape. He is mesmerized and I can see the reflection of flames in his eyes. My mom appears just in time and steers my dad away from the swirling fire. I wonder how he managed to get away from my mom. There is a huge grin on his face.

"Save me now Jesus", he yells at no one in particular, "or are you to afraid to show yourself?"

People look around but turn back to the swirling fire and pretend nothing happened. My dad grabs the whiskey bottle on the table next to him and takes a big swig. Is no one going to do anything?

"Come on, I'm waiting for you Jesus. I will fight you."

I take him inside to drink some water and sober up. I feel bad. He has been looking forward to this for months. I walk back out to the fire to watch Rachel finish the fire twirling. My plan is to join her next year juggling flaming pins. It would be epic. I already have the juggling thing down. I even tried to earn money off my skills when I went to Boston for a weekend. I put a hat down in the middle of the square and had the vision of people walking by and putting a dollar in. With so many people putting money in the hat I would be rich in no time and be at least able to pay for a flight home. It didn't quite work out. I didn't earn any money and was arrested for not having a license to perform.

I got more claps when I was arrested than for my jiggling skills. As I sat in the police station I realized that I needed to work on my skills but with practice I could really entertain people. I have only tried to light the pins on fire once to juggle them but I started a small fire in the basement and the plastic shoes melted. My parents banned me from juggling fire in the house again. I don't see what the big deal is. The old dusty red couch and the stripped carpeting were asking to be burned. Of course, there had to be a better way than dosing the pins in gasoline and taking a match to them.

After the fire dancing it is time for the fire walking. For this ritual the fire is dwindled down and the coals are raked out. I am really excited for this. Fire Walking is a ritual that has been around for centuries. Think about a world without fire. When we were cavemen hefting spears and scrawling on cave walls fire played a powerful role in society. It was a source of warmth and we started to diversify our diet. Also, people had a great respect for the power of fire and walking on it showed that we could overcome our fears and limitations. The top men in the tribe would assert their dominance by showing their inner strength by walking on the flaming hot coals.

Ironically, fire walking has been a staple of many religious ceremonies. Homas is an ancient fire ritual, which includes fire walking. It stems from Vedic science. It has something to do with the unconscious and awareness about the world around us, but it includes fire walking so it has to be badass. In today's society, fire walking is done for several reasons. Sometimes it is done as an initiation process when entering into a religion. I want to show Rebecca how brave I can be. I will take a slow walk across the hot coals and it will be my moment. As I watch the coals darken I mentally prepare myself. Becca will be so impressed.

I am suddenly taken out of my fantasy when a marshmallow hits me in the side of the head. I turn around to see the neighborhood wild child, aptly nicknamed Denise from Denise the Menace, doubled over in laughter. He even has the same haircut and a Nerf Gun he shoots at cars driving around the neighborhood. I barely have time to think before another marshmallow bounces off my nose. Man, that actually hurt. I wonder who gave the little hellion a marshmallow gun and where his parents are, although they are even worse. As a wise man once said Insanity breeds Insanity. The father is always challenging my dad to feats of strength like wood chopping contests and wheelbarrow races. The rules are simple. The fathers have the sons put in the wheelbarrows and they wheel them to where two stumps await with axes already laid out. After chopping ten pieces of wood and neatly staking them in a pile the sons get back in the wheelbarrow and there is a race to the finish line.

A date was actually set for the contest and invitations were sent out to the entire neighborhood. There was months of trash talking and my mother had to remind my father he was a grown man. Luckily, it rained heavily the day of the contest and a makeup date hasn't been set yet. For her part, the mother calls the house all the time just to tell my mom that hellion child is better than me. For her credit my mom refuses to participate. I have no idea what is wrong with these people but for some reason they are obsessed with competition and claiming they are better than my family. Even for this party, they kept insisting we have a contest to determine the best soup because the one they brought was clearly superior.

After hitting me with another marshmallow, the hellion ducks behind a tree for a second while I grit my teeth. The kid has been taunting me the entire night, following me around and challenging me to either pool or ping-pong. I decided I was the best at ping-pong and I figured he would stop harassing me if I played him and, of course, he won. A big crowd of kids attending the party formed and chanted his name. After every point the crowd cheered and when he started to beat me handily I got really nervous. Man, this guy was a genius; tricking me into playing a sport he knew he was superior at. I have to give the kid some credit. He beat me three times in a row and I got embarrassed. The kid has been bragging about it ever since, following me around so I can't even turn around without running into him. He kept saying he was a better than me and the wins proved it. At first it was cool and I admired his confidence. After a while, however it got super annoying and I have been trying to avoid him ever since. I haven't seen him in awhile until now. He comes out from behind the tree fully loaded and ready to shoot.

"Hey Loser, I bet you're too much of a wuss to walk on the fire."

"It's not a…"

A marshmallow hits me in the eye.

"…competition."

Okay, that one really hurt. Is a twelve-year-old tormenting me? I look at Becca and she is laughing. I am hit with another marshmallow and I have had just about enough. He starts dancing around in the snow pointing at the fire.

"I will cross the coals so many times my feet blister. You are too scared to even try."

Becca laughs again. I can't believe she thinks this is funny but she does speak up on my behalf.

"Kid, why would you want to hurt your feet. That's really dumb."

"Not as stupid as proving I am better than your really stupid boyfriend"

Aha, I have him now. Becca smiles and delivers the knockout punch.

"Uh, yeah I agree. That is stupid."

The kid realizes he made a mistake and just stares at me. He walks away but I know he will be back. We have been dating for a while but in that moment I knew I had someone special in Becca. The moment seemed right and without thinking I blurted out something I had wanted to say.

"I love you."

Becca turns around and looks at me. She doesn't say anything for a second and I am about to panic when she smiles and touches my shoulder.

"Aw honey, I love you too."

I hold her close and am about to kiss her when another marshmallow hits me in the side of the head. I turn to see the kid crouched behind a tree.

"Oh common, she loves you out of pity. She knows how much better I am than you."

"I am not participating."

"Is that because you are scared? It's okay, you can admit it."

"Why you little..."

I am about to lose it when Becca turns me around and kisses me. Little Hellion child calmly takes his marshmallow gun and walks back to the house. I can't believe he ruined my moment but in the end I was able to one up him. Oddly enough, his way of showing affection is very similar to his way of showing his devilish side. He had a big crush on a girl in his class at school so he continuously pelted her with spitballs and actually bought his marshmallow gun just for her. I had imagined what it would be like when I finally told Kristin I loved her and in my head it is a truly magical moment. I thought it would be romantic but that beast of a boy has managed to taint it. That kid has insulted my honor and he deserves a well timed glove slap if nothing else. If this was the old west we would have a duel but I still refuse to stoop to his level. I don't need to burn my feet to be secure with my honor and respectability. I am not going to be intimidated and he should answer for his crime.

The time of the big event has finally arrived. Everyone gathers around the raked out coals in silence. No one is volunteering to go first. Usually it is my dad but he is in the house sleeping it off. Last year his feet actually got burned. If not done correctly fire walking can be dangerous. I am trying to muster the courage, when hellion child stoically walks through the crowd and stands in front of the coals. He cleans his feet off and stands poised at the edge of the fire. He is flexing and showing off to the crowd. This is getting ridiculous. Becca leans over and whispers in my ear laughing.

"Look, he's really going to do it. Maybe he is better than you."

I truly can't believe it. He can't do it before me. That is just wrong. He takes a bow and a hush falls over the people around the fire. He gives me a broad smile and then slowly walks across. I don't know if it's bravery or stupidity but when he reaches the middle he turns and points a finger at me.

"Beat this Sam."

Everyone turns to me. His brother, equally hellish, is cheering him on.

"Ohhh, no he didn't. It is getting crazy up in here. Sounds like a challenge."

A little kid has called me out. Do I really have a choice now but to take on this kid. He finishes walking across the coals, turns around and walks back across. All childish behavior aside, I am impressed. Despite the large crowds at this event, over 50 at the least, only about ten people a year fire walk. They usually scamper across and I have never seen anyone walk as slow as he did. After walking back across he immediately runs up to me.

"I walked across twice. You can't even do it once. Admit that you are too scared and in front of everyone bow to me so we finally know who is better."

He starts dancing around me and waving his arms. I refuse to bow to him.

"Look, I'm Sam. I suck at everything. A six-year-old girl is less afraid than I am. I want to do it but I'm just a gigantic baby."

I have had just about enough.

"I am not scared. That is preposterous."

"Oh, look at me, I use big words when I'm scared."

I am way above this. There is no way I am giving in too such childish behavior. I spot the kids father in the crowd. He has a gigantic grin on his face and I suddenly realize the father is encouraging the atrosoius behavior of the little hellion.

"Come on son, show him who is the boss. Kick his ass!"

I can't believe this.

"No one is fighting here…"

The kid kicks me hard in the shin.

"Ow, what the…"

He kicks me a second time.

"Stop, stop. Why are you kicking my shins? This is getting silly."

"What's silly is your wussiness."

"Kid, that's not even a word. Look, I will not stoop to your level."

"And here come the short jokes. I may be short but I am metaphysically bigger than you."

"Uh, I think you mean metaphorically."

"Aha, but I am physically short not phorically short. Apparently the English language eludes you. "

"Okay, but you're are not even using a metaphor, so... Although I guess I said you used one so that was me being dumb...You know what, let's just forget it."

This is getting way out of hand. I pause and look around. Everyone is staring at us not saying a word. Kristin, completely silent until now, reaches up and touches me on the shoulder.

"Honey, you're getting beaten by a ten year old. Maybe you should just walk on the fire and get it over with."

"Honey, first of all he is twelve. I know because he said when was ten he was beating up high schoolers, dating college chicks, and riding a Harley to school."

Wouldn't you know it the damn kid kicks me again really hard. I reach down to massage my bruised shin as the kid crosses his arms. He sneers.

"And now I can tell people I beat up a college guy."

I realize I have no choice at this point. I could be stubborn and refuse to walk on the fire because I really have nothing to prove and giving in to this scoundrel sickens me. On the other hand, if I do it maybe this obnoxious nuisance will leave me alone. Also, I do legitimately care Kristin thinks. I want her to see me as brave. I take a deep breath and look at the kid.

"Alright, I'll walk on the coals. Step aside and let me show you how it is done."

People cheer as I take off my shoes and clean off my feet. I stand on the edge of the coals intensely staring at the other end.

My heart is pounding. I am really nervous. I am worried that I will hurry across in only a step or two or that I will chicken out and jump off in the middle. It really takes strong mental fortitude to take the first step and nerves take over after this. I try to clear my mind and calm the pounding of my heart. I put my foot out over the coals but feel the heat and pull it back. My concentration is broken by the hellian standing right next to me. I jump at the sound of his voice.

"See, you can't do it. All this talk about how you don't need to prove yourself and yet you hesitate. You know what everyone is thinking. Prove to everyone you are not a failure."

I stretch my feet out over the coals once more. I hesitate for a brief second before I gingerly take my first step. I can feel the heat spread out from my heal to my toes. I want to run across quickly like I usually do but I know I have to walk to make sure the kid stops talking smack. I take a quick step. It's mind over matter really, and my mind is already starting to lose. I have to dig deep. I take a third step and a fourth and I am already halfway across. I look through the swirling smoke to the end of the coals. The kid is grinning at me.

"That fire sure is hot. Scamper across and it will all be over."

I stand in the middle of the coals alternately picking my feet up so they don't burn.

"You wish. I will have you know my feet feel fine"

The little hellion frowns at me. I confidently finish walking the rest of the way, turn around, and casually walk back. The kid looks dejected but still walks over to me and crosses his arms.

"Well done grasshopper, but this proves absolutely nothing. Let's make this more interesting. I challenge you to a series of intellectual and physical battles."

"Okay, this is getting absurd."

"The winner gets ultimate bragging rights. It would also be cool if we could get some symbol of validation. I'm sure the neighborhood would come together and chip in to get a trophy or a prize."

"Why would they do that?"

"Uh duh, it's going to be an exciting battle and they are rooting for me."

"Yeah, I don't think so."

"Okay, winner gets your girlfriend."

I look down at him. He is really close to crossing the line here.

"No way little man. You can't say things like that, got it?"

Hellion child crosses his arms. I set my jaw and widen my eyes. He uncrosses his arms and kicks the ground.

"Fine."

"I don't understand why you care so much. Why are you constantly competing with me?"

Hellian child stops. His broad mocking grin has disappeared.

"Competition is a way to prove myself to you."

This is the first glimpse of humanity I have seen from the kid in quite some time and I have to wonder why. He has been aggressively competing with me for the last several years and I have never really gotten an explanation.

"Why does everything have to be a competition though? Why do you feel the need to prove yourself?"

"I like the challenge. It's fun and you're a worthy opponent."

Wow, I had no idea. I suddenly feel bad for the kid. I have totally misjudged him. I am touched that he would look up to me.

"Really, you actually respect me."

Former hellion kid smiles

"Don't let it go to your head. I'm still better than you."

He squarely kicks me in the shin one last time and runs into the house. The Solstice party is a big success. My dad slept it off and as the fire started to dwindle late into the night he came out once again wearing the crab hat and had a few laughs with the remaining partygoers. He even managed to walk on the coals before they had dwindled too far. What I always love about the party is I hardly get to see some of the people that come. Although I was mostly preoccupied with former Hellian child, it was fun catching up. I look forward to next year's solstice party and whatever craziness comes with it. Becca had a great time at the party and our relationship was very strong after that. I am impressed that after the crab hat and seeing me being pelted by marshmallows she is still invested in the relationship. I will always fondly remember the moment I told her I loved her. It is one of those magical moments in my life that I will never forget. As for hellian child he continues to pester me despite the respect.

When I came home for Christmas break he was waiting for me with water balloons and a Nerf gun. Right then and there he declared war on my entire family and me. Dressed head to toe in camouflage and war paint he struck a heroic pose and stated dramatically: "Things just got real. You don't want it to get personal, well things just got personal." I reluctantly embraced the threat knowing he would not leave me alone until I was soaking wet and had been continuously pelted with foam arrows. The kid is relentless and just does not stop. After several days of warfare to appease the kid much to my surprise he went away for a while. When he finally rang the doorbell after about a week he asked me if I wanted to play a game of pool. His competiveness is still there but he is now quite gracious and I enjoy his calmer side.

MY BUCKET LIST

A lot of people make lists of what they want to do before they die, or kick the bucket for lack of a better expression. My grandmother made such a list when my grandfather passed away and has been trying to follow it ever since. Last year she took a weeklong trip to Paris and walked on the Great Wall of China a week later. She called it the trip of a lifetime. She always wished she had learned how to play the guitar so at the age of 82 she spent hours learning and at a talent show at her nursing home won first place for playing the theme song to her favorite show, "Jake and the Fat Man." I highly recommend it. She was up against stiff competition, including a tap dancing fool who strained his back halfway through his performance and was disqualified. Luckily the ambulance for him was close by when another contestant singing her heart out stumbled and fell of the stage straining to hit a high note. There weren't any more talent shows after that.

For a brief time my grandmother was in a band called "**** you Death" made up of my grandmother, an older gentleman on drums, and a senile old woman who thought she was back in her High School music class. Sometimes she would bang on a keyboard while other times she mumbled gibberish into a microphone as lead vocals. I asked her once why she had joined the band. She claimed she was not in a band but if I knew anyone that needed a member she would love to do it.

She then called me cute and asked me out to the Senior Prom. The songs the band sings I would label as depressing such as their melancholy love ballad "My family just pulled the plug", the always uncomfortable and sometimes graphic "The cancer is eating away at my organs", and the one the nursing home banned from ever being played again "I'm already dead inside". Some of the more intimate entries on my grandmother's bucket list including having sex with Wayne Newton overlooking the Grand Canyon and having a romantic carriage ride through central park with the members of the Blue Man Group are still in the works. No. 12 on her list, beating up Carrot Top, is also pending. I told her I would help and if nothing else I had to be there in person.

I hope you have enjoyed reading the awkward moments from my life. It has been therapeutic to write them down and reflect on what they mean for me. Hopefully I will get to pass them on some day to my family. Life experiences are endless and new chapters are constantly being written. It has been a labor of love bringing these stories to life and I need an adequate ending to put everything in perspective. In lieu of such an ending I have decided to share my own Bucket List with you. I say it is never too early to make your own list. There are things we all want to accomplish sometime in our lives and writing them down serves as a constant reminder that life is out there waiting for us but we have to take the initiative to go get it. I decided to focus on only a couple of entries on my list that are really important to me. The entire list, expanding everyday, follows this one.

1) Buy an Island

Yes, it is very expensive but it would be so awesome. I want to find a secluded one that is relatively undeveloped but still has the potential for all the amenities including running water, electricity and satellite T.V. It would be tropical with white sandy beaches and coral reefs surrounding the island. The perfect day would be getting up early to enjoy fresh coconut and pineapple from the trees surrounding my island bungalow, fishing in the morning to catch fish for dinner, spending the afternoon lying on the beach relaxing with a Caribbean martini, snorkeling until early evening, and as the light disappears building a fire and cooking the fish I had caught earlier that day. It would be amazing. It would be my own private hideaway to get away from it all. All the pressures of the world melt away when you have your own secluded sanctuary. When I get married it will be the perfect vacation home. It is also my goal to but an island because to do so I would have to have lots of disposable income. If I have tons of money I would install a fountain in the front of my island bungalow featuring a gold statue of myself. That might be excessive and a tad egotistical.

I, of course, would not tell anyone about the island so it would be a perfect hideout. At this point I would be an international super spy engaged in espionage for several different world powers. Built into the island is a secret lair where a team of top field agents train and a tactical team of my choosing equips me with the latest in technology and high tech weaponry. With it doubling as a quant family home, the island would be the perfect cover. After retirement as a super spy I would enjoy family life but remain a bounty hunter for hire. Several years ago I went on a cruise with my family and visited one particular tropical private island that was so serene and I would have been content to stay there until another cruise ship came and picked me up. From the cruise ship I could get an ice chest of beer, tons of specialty prepared food, and all my belongings and it would have been the best vacation ever.

I told our escort I would like to buy the island and wrote him a check for $50. I figured he knew the owner and would put a good word in for me. He said he would gladly take the money but he wasn't even sure if it was for sale. I may have to use my spy skills to figure out if this is indeed true. I vowed right then and there that someday one would be mine.

2) Acquire a Superpower

It would have to be something badass like invisibility, teleportation, or the ability to read minds. It would be awesome to be invisible because then I could go wherever I wanted. I would realistically use the power to freak people out. I would go to where someone works and mentally pester them the entire day. They would take a sip of coffee, turn around for a second, and when they turn back around it would be moved to somewhere else on their desk.

Either that or I would drink it while they weren't looking and when they turn around the mug is empty. The next time the coffee would be replaced by a cup of water or the mug would disappear entirely. When they have eventually convinced themselves they aren't crazy I would do other things like take their computer when they were on break and put it somewhere else in the office so they would have to go find it. Maybe they would blame someone else in the office so I could just sit back and watch the chaos I had caused. It would provide hours of free entertainment. I wonder if my arch nemesis, Robert, has an office job. If so, I really need to get on this invisibility thing.

Another great thing about being invisible is you can go anywhere. Never again would you need tickets to go to a sporting event, you could slip right by security and without being noticed gain access to the most secure areas on earth, and you could appear out of nowhere to freak out your friends. Teleportation would be neat because I realistically spend a good amount of time on the way to places. If you were invisible and could teleport you could literally go anywhere in an instant and do everything without being noticed. It would be awesome. I was not born with powers so I would have to get them from an outside source. I could be dropped in a vat of radioactive goo, be the byproduct of a freak accident that somehow altered my DNA, or be exposed to large amounts of radiation.

If I knew I could gain awesome superpowers I would gladly spend hours standing in front of a microwave. My question is, if turtles exposed to radioactive ooze become nearly 100 times their original size, gain the ability to speak, gain increased intelligence and innate martial arts ability, what would happen to a person. If exposed I could potentially be bigger than a house, be the smartest person on the planet, and kick major ass. Man, where is some radioactive ooze when you need it. I also wonder why when rats are dropped in radioactive ooze they are automatically better at karate than turtles. I also wonder why the same radioactive ooze gives the same beings different personalities. If I was "accidentally" dropped in a vat of radioactive goo I could become a science driven intellectual or a partying bad boy who loves pizza.

Don't confuse this with wanting to be a superhero. That is way too much work and I don't look good in stretchy pants. I would help some people here or there but in no way would I make it a profession. I do; however, plan on running around town in a cape revealing hidden secrets and causing chaos. After this I would immediately run away. I would be called "Awkward Man." I imagine a couple sitting at a very nice restaurant one evening. I run up wearing a cape and pronounce boldly: "He's cheating on you." and then run away. Two best buds are hanging out. I run up, point at one of the guys and shout: "He's imagined you naked." I then immediately run away. Two girls are sitting at a café gossiping. I run up, point at one of the girls and loudly announce: "She hates your new haircut". After a long pause I would uncomfortable shout: "She thinks you are slutty" and then run away.

I know it could be viewed as mean but I'd like to think I would be doing some good. It would make people confront issues that would have been ignored otherwise. 'Awkward Man' becomes a symbol of honesty and the city honors me with a medal of appreciation. Of course with the success of 'Awkward Man' there would no doubt be marketing demands. My likeness would appear on lunch boxes and there would be a series of action figures. A Saturday morning cartoon with some bizarre villains thrown in would become a critical success and, of course, that would spin off into a series of movies starring my favorite actor, Bill Murray. Bill, if you are reading this, I need you to commit to this. Call me. As long as it is badass, I definitely want a superpower.

3) Gain the ability to breathe fire

Breathing fire would be so awesome. I have always been fascinated with dragons. In a former life I am convinced I was a dragon sitting in a castle guarding a pile of golden treasure. There is an intricate maze potential dragon slayers have to navigate to get to the castle. There are booby traps, challenging riddles, and even mythic creatures that must be defeated along the way. It would be complete with a David Bowie look-a-like wearing white spandex and holding an owl. He would be my worthy sidekick, confusing hopeful treasure hunters on their journey. The legend of my greatness would be unmatched. New challengers to slay me and take the treasure would see the bodies of brave warriors far tougher than them lining the walls of the castle. Dragons were a huge part of my childhood dreamscape. They transported me to far off lands and remarkable adventures.

If I could truly breathe fire, if nothing else I would be invited to parties to show off my ability. At the Winter Solstice Party I would show up the fire twirler. You can twirl fire, big deal. I can breathe fire. With a tilt of my head flames would come out of my mouth and I could light the fire in an instant. Breathing fire has so many practical uses. If I need to light a sparkler on the Fourth of July I don't need a match and can light it at a safe distance just by opening my mouth. If someone needs to light their pipe I can do it in an instant.

I have to be careful though. If I get careless I could singe off their eyebrows. A group of buds and me are roasting marshmallows over the fire when the wind picks up and blows out the fire. No problem, I can either light the logs in an instant or they can put the marshmallows in from of my face and I can cook them to golden perfection. If I am on a hot date and want to set the mood I can dim the lights and within seconds light all the candles in the room. Realistically I could burn down villages and terrorize the countryside so no one would want to mess with me and I would have lots of unspeakable power. I would just tell people they don't want to see me when I am angry. It would be so badass. On the other hand, I could use my power for good and when anyone needed to light something but didn't have a match or a lighter I would be there in a heartbeat to work my magic.

4) Fight Chuck Norris

Understand that in no way am I saying I can defeat Chuck Norris. He has an eighth degree black belt and has been kicking ass for years. He has been competing in martial arts competitions for years and has become a legendary fighter.

In his prime, he could hold his own and possibly win a fight with Bruce Lee. Speaking as a very cheap man, I would pay thousands of dollars to see a no holds bar cage fight between the two. It would be so epic the world would literally stop and hold its collective breath. Even then the excitement and tension would be so palpable the world couldn't handle it all and commit planetic suicide. People just assume only animals can die at their own hand but according to scientific fact planets become easily stressed and merely fade from existence when they feel too much pressure. What do you think happened to Pluto? Scientists didn't demote it from being a planet. Pluto just couldn't take being picked on as the smallest planet in the universe and cracked under the pressure.

Naturally, Chuck Norris has way more martial arts experience than I do. The only martial arts experience I have is breaking a board in half when I was ten. I still have the board dated and signed by my instructor. It was a proud moment for me. Unfortunately, it was the only class I ever took so I never got a belt. I have never been in a fight before either. When I was five I stole a kid's ice cream cone and he cried but I quickly gave it back to him and no punches were thrown. Robert and I always had our spats but the tension never led to fisticuffs.

I would have to train really hard to even stand a chance against someone with half the ability of Chuck Norris. I would take inspiration from Rocky and punch slices of deli meat to improve my upper body strength. I would try and catch stray dogs and cats to improve my agility. I would grow a wicked mustache to amuse and confuse my opponent. To be extra distracting my facial hair would continuously change shape. One minute I have a well-groomed goatee and then in an instant it morphs into mutton chops. To even stand toe to toe with the man would be such an honor. Despite the epic beating

I would undoubtedly endure, I could say I had the bravery to fight. It would officially prove how badass I am. In arguments I could officially say: "Oh yeah, well I fought Chuck Norris." I wonder if I write a letter officially challenging him to fight he would do it. He must have an agent I can contact.

5) Clone myself

I admit it; I am a very lazy man. If laziness were a disease I wouldn't stand a chance. Ironically the cure for laziness is not being lazy but laziness is the reason I have the disease in the first place. My favorite day is those lazy Sundays where it is socially acceptable to sit around not fully clothed on your couch all day watching sports and drinking beer. If there were more of me instead of having to get off the couch I could have one clone bring me a beer, another fluff the pillow, and another bring me the remote. With multiple clones I literally would not have to move the entire day. Each one would be slightly different. There could be an alternate me that was really dedicated. I would send him off to work where he could do a great job, gain the respect of his colleagues, and then the real me would swoop in periodically to take all the credit.

In the meantime I could do other things on my bucket list like figuring out how to breathe fire. If I had multiple disposable clones I could have them do hands on research to discover how this would be possible. If one of the clones gets burned in an unfortunate gasoline accident I have tons more to take his place. There is an ethical dilemma though. In all consciousness could I let something die that looks exactly like me in every way? How would I feel if I put a clone in real danger, both emotionally and physically? These are questions to ponder.

I would definitely have a suave clone because frankly my lady skills are somewhat lacking. He would meet the girl, sweep her off her feet, and set up a first date. I would then come in to start the relationship because I find once I get past the asking out stage I am fine. Of course some clones wouldn't work out. If a clone was just as lazy as I am I would sit around yelling at it to be more productive and nothing would be accomplished. Another problem is if I can clone myself I assume the technology is readily available. It would weird me out and frustrate me if later I found out I had been talking to a clone or even dating a clone. The sociological implications alone are mind-boggling. Plus, we have the technology to clone other animals but why stop at a sheep. If we cloned bears we could repopulate the area around my house and old man Freeman would have something to hunt. I still don't understand why I can't be his wisecracking sidekick.

6) Have sex on the moon

I have always wanted to go to the moon. To bounce around on the lunar surface would be amazing. I would have jumping contests with fellow astronauts to see who could bounce the highest. I would have to come up with something historic to say when I first stepped foot on the surface. I was thinking "Screw mankind, that is one step for me" or "Bring on the aliens." I have a great idea for a movie. A high school nerd constantly gets picked on in school. No one in the school respects him and the girl of his dreams has just turned him down for a date after he finally mustered up the courage to ask her.

His family life is a mess and his parents barely pay any attention to him. The only place he fits in and is accepted is the school Chess Club. Then a cunning and diabolical alien race takes over the galaxy. They are planning to destroy earth and there is nothing that will stand in their way. In an ironic twist of fate the alien race loves the game of chess and decries if anyone on Earth can beat the best chess player of the alien race Earth will be sparred along with the rest of the universe. The kid that no one believes in is the only one to take up the challenge and the fate of the universe rests on his shoulders.

It is a coming of age tale and is inspirational as well. I would totally watch that movie. Regardless, I would love to go to the moon. The view alone would be awesome. I figure if I can have sex on the moon it would be because of two possible scenarios: either that I am an astronaut on an expedition or am working on a lunar base. If I am an astronaut the suits would be a problem but I figure if we had some sort of breathing apparatus it could be done. If not a breathing apparatus we could be inside a giant dome. I would be famous for the coolest first ever and year's later kids in middle school and high school would know my name and idolize me. I would become not only famous but also infamous. If I were in a lunar base it would not be as cool as the actual surface of the moon of course to have sex in zero gravity would be neat. It would definitely be interesting.

7) Go scuba diving on the great barrier reef

This is something I have always wanted to do. When I was a kid I was obsessed with the ocean. I would go to the aquarium and spend hours staring at the penguins. They probably thought I was really creepy. If I was in an enclosure and some random penguin came every day to stare at me I would feel very uncomfortable. I would be like: "How dare you penguin for staring at me. I understand I am cute and fun to look at but I have needs. I need my privacy." I would be really uncomfortable if a cow came to see me at a zoo and I was eating a steak. When I was a kid I also drew elaborate drawings of underwater sanctuaries for stick figures. The stick figures swim with the fish and conduct under water experiments. Of course, one of the boy stick figures falls in love with a beautiful mermaid. I used to think that would be awesome.

I really don't understand why people would be attracted to mermaids though. I would like to swim underwater and never be out of breath too but don't mermaids have fish parts on the entire lower part of their body if you know what I mean. The alternative is not a good option either, with the lower body human and the upper part of the body fish.

What I love about the ocean is its mystery and power. There are some parts of the ocean we have not reached yet and it is fun to imagine what kinds of creatures are down there. The colossal giant squid is crazy to imagine and the sightings reveal how awesome the ocean is. Imagine a squid but only an estimated 20-30 times its size. When I was a kid I was on a trip to the Outer Banks, a beach in North Carolina, and walking on a pier that extended far out onto the ocean I witnessed one of the craziest things I have ever seen. I remember hearing yelling and looked to the end of the pier to see three grown men grabbing onto a heavy duty fishing pole having the fight of their lives with whatever they had caught. After a long struggle they finally reeled in a full-grown hammerhead shark. To see it up close was amazing. It was thrashing its teeth and looked quite menacing. The two guys who had caught it threw it into a shopping cart and afraid it would bite them they had to continuously stab it until it finally stopped thrashing about. I believe we have to respect the power of the sea. One of the best examples of this can be seen in the poem below:

I USED TO LOVE THE SEA

I used to love the sea; it's placid tranquility.
All that changed one icy December.
I stand in a small vessel traveling into the sunset,
A favorite pastime since I was a lad.
Surrounding me is a small crew, paddling with delight

NICHOLAS KERESZTURY

Despite the crowd around me
I feel like I am the last man on earth
The waves rock the boat just for me
The sunset illuminates my face alone
The sea hugs me with a passion I can't explain…

Without warning the boat rocks violently
Pushed up by an unknown force
I topple over the side;
Grabbing only air on the way down
I hit the water in a tangle of limbs

I surface; I am in shock
The painful cold has gripped me
I can feel my legs tighten
I look into the distance to see
A ripple of water bearing down upon me

I stare into the eyes of the great beast.
It has no pupils, just two black fixed circles
There is no humanity behind the blackness,
A soulless creature prepared to eat me whole
I am nothing but unprotected flesh, a fast and easy meal.

In one ferocious bite my arm is ripped clean.
I scream in pain but mostly terror,
Seeing the water turn dark red around me.
I scream for someone to help me, to reach out their arm.
The bastards just stare at me, paralyzed by fear.

I am prepared to die; for death to call my name.
I let my body slowly sink below the surface,
Allowing the water to envelope me.
I stare up at the blood and think about salvation
I used to love the sea; it's placid tranquility

The Great Barrier Reef itself is home to so many different kinds of ocean life. It almost functions as its own ecosystem, providing a home to hundreds of creatures. It would be so beautiful to see. When I accomplish #1 on my list, buying an island, I will make sure there is a reef nearby so I can go Scuba diving. When I went on the cruise a couple years we went snorkeling in the beautiful crystal clear water around the location we were visiting and it really made me hungry to take it to the next level. Along with scuba diving on the Great Barrier Reef I also have the dream of taking a year off from life, buying a houseboat, and sailing around the world basking in my freedom. I wouldn't have to worry about anything. I would have the wind in my hair and adventure in my heart. I would explore all the places I stopped and have wonderful escapades with people I had just met.

8) Have a woman or women throw their panties on stage after my performance

I have never actually seen this happen and it kind of weirds me out because doesn't that mean the girl would have to bring the underwear with them. I'm not really sure what they are trying to accomplish either. It would be great if the panties had a phone number attached or a nice note saying how much they liked the performance, but otherwise it's a waste of perfectly good underwear. You also don't want to be the only one to throw underwear because then you look like a stalker. It doesn't really work for men either. It would be socially unacceptable if I threw my boxers on stage after a Spice Girls concert.

I have heard legends of performers getting this treatment. A friend of mine is in a band and he would get women planted in the audience to throw some on stage once the band is finished with their final song. He claims the crowd responds really well when it happens and it makes talent scouts think the band has a loyal following. It also doesn't hurt if members of the band are viewed as sex symbols. As we have seen recently someone with absolutely no talent can make it on looks alone. I'd like to think I could do the same but I'm not sure. I figure if you take moderately attractive and add electrifying stage presence you could get a lot of attention. In the case of some lead singers for popular bands it doesn't really matter if they are unattractive.

I am destined to be on stage. I love to perform stand-up comedy and while I am very raw I do want to find a comedy club I can be a regular at. It would be so awesome. Who knows, maybe I can parlay it into a real career and do stand-up comedy around the country. It would be so awesome. I figure if panties are thrown at me it's because of one of two reasons: either my hot girlfriend really loves me and is showing me her undying support or I have reached the pinnacle of my talent. Either way I am made and it is definitely a goal I want to work towards. Along with stand-up comedy I also want to act. I love being on stage in a crowded theatre with nothing but the audience and me. It gives me a thrill that nothing else gives me. My ultimate goal is to do a stage show that no one has ever seen before and would go down as legendary. I would be the MC, of course, participating in the extravaganza as well as introducing all of the acts.

It would include death defying mystical magic acts and illusions, the world's best juggling acts, special guests being pied in the face, comedy from the best stand-ups in the business, and as much audience participation as possible. The ending of the show would fulfill two other entries on my list. A gigantic cake would be wheeled out onto the stage. Around the cake there would be a show stopping dance number and at the end all the dancers would throw money out into the audience as it also rained from the ceiling. At the same time I would pop out of the cake announcing the end of the show. If there is one thing I learned from life it is you should never expect panties but if a couple were thrown onto stage to boot it would be the best night ever. I know I dream big but anything is possible. Having panties thrown on the stage after my performance is a key entry on my list.

9) Get Married and Start a Family

I actually like going to weddings. They are festive and I am quite the dancer if I do say so myself. I am really excited for my friend's wedding coming up in the fall. It is happening on my birthday so I have been given certain allowances. I will be juggling during the reception. I actually learned at my cousin's wedding when crazy uncle Erne taught me by juggling rolls. It got uncomfortable when he screamed 'let's kick it up a notch' and lit the rolls on fire. The tablecloth almost went up in flames and the burns on his hands took several weeks to heal. I suspect he wanted to create a commotion though. It happened during the best man's speech and even though he wasn't that close with the family in his mind he was the better man and deserved to give the speech.

I learned that day that unless you have special gloves it is a bad idea to juggle flaming juggling balls. Since then Uncle Ernie doesn't come to any of the family gatherings. I'm not really sure what happened to him. I also have the go-ahead to jump out of a cake. My plan is to express my congratulations popping out of the cake singing their favorite song. It will be magical. Don't worry dear reader the wedding cake will be separate and kept intact. Popping out of a cake will also accomplish one of my entries on the more extensive bucket list.

FULL BUCKET LIST

1) **Live in an underwater house**
2) **Go on an African safari**
   I figure even if I kill a small rodent I can say I was a badass and shot down some big game. Logically, if I were a small nut a field mouse would be big to me. I would go back to my small home made out of grass and mount the mouse on the wall in my den.
3) **Have a pet monkey**
4) **Clone Myself**
5) **Fire a mini-gun**
6) **Meet an Alien**
7) **Discover multiple parallel universes**
   There could be one where dinosaurs never went extinct or plastic was never invented. The possibilities are endless.
8) **Blow up a building**
9) **Shoot a bad guy**
10) **Gain the ability to breath fire**
11) **Ride a motorcycle**
   Preferable I could jump 50 trucks through multiple rings of fire wearing a blindfold and a straight jacket. Beat that Evil Knieval.
12) **Learn how to surf**
13) **In my spare time become a juggling street performer**

14) Become part of a traveling theatre and/or comedy troupe

This would really satisfy two entries on my list, being part of a theatre or comedy group and traveling around the country.

15) Jump out of a cake

16) Become a popular radio personality

17) Dunk a basketball

Whether I have to drop out of a helicopter or wear a monkey suit and jump on a mini trampoline I will make it happen, physics and mad hops be damned.

18) Have sex on the moon

19) See Mr. Kelvin smile, if only for a second

20) Become an outdoors survivalist

I am not saying I want to live in a cave and fight bears like Mr. Freeman but I wonder if I could be dropped off in the middle of nowhere and survive with nothing but a pocket knife. I went to Boy Scout camp. One summer we went on a camping trip to test our skills. The leaders purposefully didn't bring enough food and said we had to find our own food. We ate crawdads out of a stream and all got violently ill. There was some sort of lawsuit but I'm not really sure what happened with that. Regardless, I do wonder if I could do it.

21) Be a hit man for hire

22) Live in a cave

23) Get another tattoo

It's true, I do have a tattoo of Mr. Peanut breathing fire and burning down a village on my back. When I suggested it to the tattoo artist he couldn't stop laughing. I'm still not sure what he thought about the idea.

24) Get married and start a family

25) Buy a beach house

26) Write a novel

Ah, I can already cross one off. Go me! I have so many awkward stories to tell I could definitely write a second volume though.

27) Buy an island
28) Get the novel published

Man, if you are paying to read these words I feel sorry for you but I also appreciate it.

29) Go snorkeling on the great barrier reef
30) Have a child named after me
31) Fight Chuck Norris
32) Win the Nobel prize

I want to either invent something that could change the world or make a scientific breakthrough. I'd prefer discovering time travel or a portal to faraway worlds but I am open to others

33) Challenge someone to a duel
34) Travel to India and ride an elephant
35) Gain a superpower
36) Have a holiday named after me

National 'Nicholas Keresztury' day would be a nationwide celebration of everything awesome. Everyone would get a day off to contemplate my greatness and my everlasting legacy. Customary activities for this special day would include carnival festivities all over the country, balloons, cake, and lot of fun.

37) Eat poisonous blowfish
38) Go to the Super Bowl
39) Build a secret tunnel
40) Chill with my favorite comic actor, Bill Murray

My plan is to go to frat parties with him unannounced, do shots, and leave with people wondering if that just happened. Maybe we could go ghost hunting or go to Japan so I could find myself. In my perfect groundhog day Bill would definitely be involved.

41) Sit at the desk of the President of the United States
42) Discover buried treasure

43) Compete in the World Series of Poker
44) Invent a new alcoholic beverage

  It would be so awesome if someone could walk into a bar and say; "I'll have a Nicholas Keresztury" I would be sweet, smooth, never bitter, and extra delicious.

45) Have a woman/ women throw their panties on stage after my performance
46) Travel to Egypt
47) Have an enthusiastic personal assistant to help me in all my crazy schemes
48) Ride in a hot air balloon
49) Perform a one manned show dressed as Mr. Peanut

  I could juggle or tell jokes. I engage in witty banter with my funny sidekick, my young nephew lil' peanut. Near the end of the show I do an elaborate magic trick where he is tied up in chains inside a cylinder with a crushing mechanism that threatens to squash him into dust. Suddenly, he disappears before the audience's very eyes. When I ask what happened to lil' peanut my stage assistant comes out wheeling a big jar of peanut butter. Admittedly, the joke is rather dark.

50) Roll around in a big pile of money
51) Play in a rock band
52) Open a comedy club
53) Tame a wild horse

  I wonder if I could train it to do tricks like sit on command or jump through hoops of fire. It could be the opening act for rodeos across the country and I would finally get a chance to show off my cowboy skills.

54) See Bigfoot
55) Climb Mount Everest
56) Go ghost hunting in an abandoned and haunted former insane asylum
57) Live life to the fullest each and every day

Well, that just about sums it up. We all have awkward stories to tell. I was just dumb enough to write them down and share them with the world. The one thing I can say is if you're undecided about what you want to do with your life you are not alone. Don't let others dictate the path you take, and always do it for yourself. Your dreams are important. Look at it this way: your mother always lectured you to read more and you've just completed an entire novel. I raise my glass to you. Also, if you are awkward like me embrace it. Trust me; we need more people like you in this world. Now, if you will excuse me I have apology letters to write to everyone I have offended writing this novel. I am going to be busy for a while and I may go bankrupt buying stationary. If you are reading this I hopefully already have your money, but could I borrow a few extra bucks?

Would you like to see your manuscript become a book?

CPSIA information can be obtained at www.ICGtesting.com
Printed in the USA
267863BV00001B/41/P